Instagram POWER

SECOND EDITION

BUILD YOUR BRAND AND REACH MORE CUSTOMERS WITH VISUAL INFLUENCE

JASON MILES

Mc
Graw
Hill
Education

New York Chicago San Francisco Athens London Madrid
Mexico City Milan New Delhi Singapore Sydney Toronto

2 3 4 5 6 7 8 9   LCR   24 23 22 21 20 19

ISBN: 978-1-260-45330-0
ISBN: 1-260-45330-8

e-ISBN: 978-1-260-45331-7
e-ISBN: 1-260-45331-6

This publication is designed to provide accurate and authoritative information in regard to the subject matter covered. It is sold with the understanding that neither the author nor the publisher is engaged in rendering legal, accounting, securities trading, or other professional services. If legal advice or other expert assistance is required, the services of a competent professional person should be sought.

> —*From a Declaration of Principles Jointly Adopted by a Committee of the American Bar Association and a Committee of Publishers and Associations*

Library of Congress Cataloging-in-Publication Data

Names: Miles, Jason, 1970- author.
Title: Instagram power : build your brand and reach more customers with visual influence / by Jason Miles.
Description: Second edition. | New York : McGraw-Hill, [2019]
Identifiers: LCCN 2018051195| ISBN 9781260453300 (alk. paper) | ISBN 1260453308
Subjects: LCSH: Internet marketing. | Social media--Marketing. | Branding (Marketing)
Classification: LCC HF5415.1265 .M537 2019 | DDC 658.8/72--dc23 LC record available at https://lccn.loc.gov/2018051195

McGraw-Hill Education books are available at special quantity discounts to use as premiums and sales promotions or for use in corporate training programs. To contact a representative, please visit the Contact Us pages at www.mhprofessional.com.

For my amazing wife and business partner,
Cinnamon, and our wonderful kids,
Jordan, Makena, and Liberty

Contents

Part I
P = PREP FOR SUCCESS

Part II
O = ORGANIZE YOUR MESSAGE

Part III
W = WOW THEM WITH EFFECTIVE MARKETING

Part IV
E = EXPAND WITH ADVERTISING AND INFLUENCERS

Part V
R = REFINE YOUR INSTAGRAM EFFORTS WITH TOOLS AND SERVICES

Acknowledgments

This book would not have been possible without the wisdom and guidance of my agent, Marilyn Allen. Marilyn, thank you for providing practical advice and encouragement. It is an honor to be your client. I'd also like to thank each of the contributors who took the time to share their Instagram insights. Your contributions made this book a joy to write. I'm also grateful for my daughter, Liberty Miles, who shows me how to use social media daily, and helped preread the manuscript. Finally, I want to thank my beautiful and talented wife, Cinnamon Miles. You are the best thing that has ever happened to me, and I love you with all my heart.

Introduction

$\mathcal{I}$ wrote the first edition to this book in the summer of 2013 for marketers and small-business owners. At the time, I felt part of my writing duty was to convince people that Instagram had a lot of merit as a tool for marketers. So naturally I packed the Introduction and first few chapters with all the recent stats I could find—all the circa 2013 proof you could ever want that Instagram was on its way to becoming a big deal. The bulk of the book was focused on how to use Instagram to conduct tried-and-true Instagram marketing in a professional way. I was right about Instagram—man, is it crazy hot. I don't need to prove that to anyone now.

Upon launch, the first edition did better than I could have hoped. But with each passing year, three things happened. First, the stats I included to argue my case for Instagram have become hilariously outdated. I should have realized prospective readers would see those stats and conclude the entire book was of no value. Oops. So much for future-proofing. Second, Instagram has added a huge amount of new functionality since 2013, much of it designed for marketers. Every time it released a new feature I said to myself, "Wow, I wish that was in my book." And third, as I have worked with students, members of my Inner Circle program, and coaching clients over the last few years, I've come to realize the power and value of a framework and step-by-step approach, so people new to marketing on Instagram can have an actionable set of tasks to get up and running quickly and easily.

When McGraw-Hill approached me to do a second edition, I was thrilled. I had my to-do list ready. I've crafted the second edition of this book to achieve the following: First, to make a clear and compelling case for Instagram as a tool for marketers and small-business owners, with an emphasis on business benefits instead of site statistics. I hope this makes the book more timeless. Second, to update the book to include strategies and tips for leveraging the latest Instagram functionality. Finally, to present to readers a more logical and memorable framework, with a step-by-step approach that anyone can follow. The framework offers a logical progression so even the most advanced Instagram users can get something out of it. I trust the insights and lessons in this book will be helpful. I'd love to see your business thrive on Instagram and beyond.

Your Tribe Is on Instagram

Can Instagram be the platform where you win big? Can it be the place where you stand out, draw a crowd, and take the leadership position you know you deserve? The place where you ring the cash register, get the customers, and find your next rock-solid marketing method? Can it work for you—even though you've tried and failed at a few other marketing efforts before? Of course it can!

Instagram is clearly working well for marketing. So the question is, *Will you make it work for you?* It's really your journey to take, your hill to climb. Your daily practice. Your vision. You're the hero of this story now, not me. If you want it, it's time to own it.

In this book you'll find 19 clear, simple, logically ordered, and easy to implement steps toward a powerful Instagram marketing strategy. It's not that big a hill to climb. Just 19 steps. It's even broken up into five sections—with a logical framework and an easy to remember acronym. You can do this!

You might already have an Instagram account going—and some marketing strategies you're using. You'll be able to skip past the set-up steps. You may even be an experienced Instagram user. Don't worry, I've got plenty for you, too, including interviews with successful Instagram marketers who will give you fantastic tips.

Don't Judge Your Success by Others

It's so easy to look at other Instagrammers and get discouraged rather than motivated. I'm guilty of it too. But *don't* do it! Don't use someone else's success to judge yourself. When we focus on comparison and competition with people who have nothing to do with us, we're only being mean to ourselves and not celebrating the other person for his or her success. Instead, walk your own path. Make yesterday's Instagram work your only yardstick of measurement. Are you doing better today than you did yesterday at leveraging the power of Instagram to build your business? Congrats—you're reading this book, so let's chalk up today as a victory! As a practical exercise, when you see successful Instagrammers in this book, celebrate with them. If you already have an Instagram account, jump on and leave a comment under their last post saying, "Congrats on all your Instagram success."

Finding Your Tribe on Instagram

In his book *Tribes*, Seth Godin compares online marketing to tribe building. The message is clear—find and serve your tribe online. Serve them with thought leadership, tips, ideas, and resources. Be the convener, encourager, humorist, and connector. If you do it well, they will follow you. Over time, your tribe will grow, they will rally in support of your efforts, and a unique bond will be formed. With a powerful tribe at your back, you'll be able to do bold things.

Godin's concept provides solid guidance to the hopeful Instagram marketer of all types. Instagram is a tribal place, where people gather around leaders and topics. Users gravitate toward individuals, brands, and personalities that they grow fond of and build an attachment to. Instagram is chaotic upon first glance, but spend a little time with it and you'll begin to see the organizing principles. You'll begin to notice how the tribes aggregate and who they rally around. You'll want a tribe of your own.

My premise for the book is simple. Your tribe is on Instagram—and if you want them to know, like, and trust you—you've got to have the Instagram marketing muscle to reach them. This book is written to give you the daily practice and strategies to find the strength. You probably won't get it all at once, but as you implement effective strategies, you'll develop the muscle, and the tribe will gather. My hope is that with these clear and easy to follow marketing tactics, step-by-step, you'll find success.

Did You Say Big Papi Loves Butterflies?

By way of quick example about the tribal nature of Instagram, while I was working on this very section of the book, I received a message from one of my coaching clients, Tony. He's the founder of a fantastic butterfly conservation effort called Raise The Migration (www .raisethemigration.com). Find him on Instagram @monarchbutterfly .garden. His message was brief, *"Big Papi's Trying To Steal My Thunder— happy face emoji."* Big Papi? I was intrigued, so I clicked the link and saw the picture (Figure I.1) of David Ortiz—Red Sox icon, 10-time Major League Baseball All-Star, massive Instagram celebrity, and yes, butterfly lover. Yes, I said Big Papi Loves Butterflies! The point? Simply this: You never know who could potentially be in your tribe. Who might be your next customer, influencer, advocate, or business partner. Learn to do the work, and let's see who shows up!

Figure I.1 Big Papi loves butterflies

Guide to the POWER Framework

Throughout the upcoming sections of this book, we'll use the acronym POWER as our guide. In each section, you'll find actionable strategies that build upon the previous section. Step-by-step, we'll put together the pieces of a professional Instagram marketing program. Here is a quick overview of what we'll cover.

P is for *Prep for Success*. In Part I you will get set up on Instagram. We'll walk through how to use all the features and understand the Instagram way. Our focus will be on creating a powerful, professional profile. I'll explain the latest Instagram improvements such as IGTV, Stories, Shoppable Posts, and more. We'll also do a crash course on hashtags, since they play a central role in Instagram marketing.

O is for *Organize Your Message*. In Part II I'll help you clarify and strengthen your visual branding on Instagram. The outcome will be a professional content strategy that you can begin using today. I'll also give you a basic marketing plan in the form of a Daily Action Checklist so you know exactly what to do each day to grow your tribe. Finally, I'll walk you through the tools and strategies related to building an Instagram support team to add fuel to your tribal fire.

W is for *Wow Them*. In Part III, I'll give you a master class in direct marketing on Instagram. We'll look at all sorts of marketing campaign methodologies to impress and attract your tribe. Whether you're a product seller, service provider, nonprofit, or local merchant, we'll break it down with step-by-step marketing actions to implement.

E is for *Expand*. In Part IV, we'll explore the tools available to help you expand and scale your Instagram marketing. We'll call in the cavalry—specifically advertisers and Influencers—effectively multiplying your marketing campaign power.

R is for *Refine*. In Part V, we'll look at tools and resources to help you continuously improve, going from Instagram marketing rookie to a true professional. We'll share resources for next steps on your journey—and discuss how we can stay connected.

This book is meant to prompt action. I'd encourage you to jump in with both thumbs. Try things. Learn by doing. Don't worry about failing. Look up the profiles of the Instagram marketers that I interview in this book, and see what they're doing. Borrow their good ideas and adapt them to your unique situation. Keep learning.

The Unlikely Journey That Brought Us Together Today

I suppose a bit about me is in order so you know who you're dealing with. I'm a nonprofit executive turned kitchen-table entrepreneur from a suburb of Seattle—the Lake Tapps area. My wife Cinnamon (@libertyjaneclothing on Instagram) and I started selling on eBay in 2008, in an act of financial desperation. During that stressful period I developed a chronic multiyear addiction to the audio version of *The 4-Hour Workweek*. My own chronology of a pathology. I listened to it over and over every few weeks, for nearly five years. It helped that I had a mind-numbing, three-hour daily commute.

By 2014, our little online effort had started to blossom. I retired from the nine-to-five job and went full-time with the family business. It was wear your pajama bottoms to work day, every day, and midday kayaking happened as needed for stress relief. Going full-time with the family business changed everything. Thanks @Timferris. Before leaving the world of suites and shiny shoes, I had been the senior VP of marketing, fundraising, and human resources for a private college in Kirkland, Washington (@northwestu). A well-paid job and one that wasn't easy to leave. I still teach Online Marketing at the school as an adjunct professor. Along the way I got an MBA, and a couple of undergraduate degrees too. I love learning!

Our small e-commerce company isn't one you've probably ever heard of, unless you're into sewing. We run Pixie Faire (@pixiefaire on Instagram), an e-commerce marketplace that sells digital sewing patterns, sewing-related video classes, and a monthly sewing club—*Sewing With Cinnamon*. Cinnamon's books have really taken off lately too, so that's a fun aspect of our work. You can find them at your local Costco, Walmart, JoAnn, Barnes & Noble, and beyond.

We're honestly not trying to be a big deal or impress people. Truth is, we'd rather hang out at the local farmers market anyway, spend time with our kids, and try to do a good job being married and working together. We care about efficient profit and minimal loss. Scaling up what we do in our own way—and being good at it.

Last month we had over 70,000 transactions through our Shopify store, www.pixiefaire.com. In the last 365 days, according to our Google Analytics, we've attracted just over 596,000 new users to Pixie Faire. Many of them via social media. Combined with our existing customers, they visited our site 2.2 million times and looked at over 14 million pages. It's tiny compared to many online sellers, but big enough to achieve our personal goals. After 10 years of doing this, we know we have our long-term competitive advantage on full lockdown in a niche that is small enough for us to monopolize, yet large enough to fund our dreams.

About my writing work? During Christmas vacation in the winter of 2011, with a desire to find a creative writing outlet, I started manically blogging about how Pinterest was revolutionizing our small business. My little wordpress.com site was the perfect place for my coffee-induced micro manifestos. I wrote something like 25 articles during that two-week vacation. Turns out my timing was pretty good. When I got back to work, I got contacted about a book deal with McGraw-Hill for *Pinterest Power*. Yeah, after just two weeks of blogging. I know, it's crazy, but true. Sometimes timing is everything.

I quickly realized that social media professionals weren't really my tribe. Nope, I'm not trying to be an Instagram or social media guru. With no disrespect to them at all. They are really nice people. I just don't fit in. Good news is, I found my tribe, small-business owners. Explaining e-commerce, Shopify, and social media to them is a blast. I love e-commerce and the process of selling online. Getting the sustainable traffic sources figured out and winning conversions. I do most of my teaching on Udemy in the e-commerce category.

Aside from work, our personal passion is growing a small ministry we started in 2010, Sew Powerful (@sewpowerful on Instagram). It's a labor of love. Something we do from a deep conviction and calling to help a group of moms in a very desperate place—Ngombe Compound, Lusaka, Zambia. What we do is create good paying jobs for the moms, grandmas, and even some dads. They work to produce items that empower academic success for the orphans and vulnerable children of their community. The kids get a better school experience, and the parents get the pride of hard work—and a mission they believe in. We make things like school uniforms, reusable feminine hygiene pads, and soap, and do gardening on a small farm to help feed the kids. At the time that this book is being written we are helping kids in 25 schools and the program is growing quickly. Last year our overhead rate was 1.35 percent and we directly helped almost 7,000 children and employed roughly 25 adults. The more our e-commerce business efforts grow, the more we can invest into the program. You can check out what we're doing on www.sewpowerful.org.

We started using Instagram for our e-commerce efforts on September 17, 2012. A year later, because of the success of my prior book, *Pinterest Power*, the first edition of this book came together. At the time, there was so little that could be done with Instagram. But it was scaling at a massive rate, and our early marketing efforts were paying off really nicely. Back then there wasn't much content online about Instagram marketing—today it's everywhere. Plus, Instagram has rolled out fantastic business-related features in the last few years. So, my job with this book is to synthesize, provide examples of concepts, and most importantly, encourage you to adapt the ideas in this book and implement them in support of your product, business, service, or nonprofit effort. My goal is your success in the real world of competitive marketing, not just to entertain you with my writing. I know you can do this!

Get Your Expansion Pack

Throughout this book I'll be regularly mentioning a series of additional resources, PDF checklists, bonus lists, case studies, and supplemental information. I'm calling it the *Expansion Pack*. You can download your free copy on a little blog I set up, www.winning.online.

You'll need the Expansion Pack because I simply couldn't pack all the content I wanted to into this book. There is so much good stuff to share about Instagram marketing! So, the Expansion Pack became my overflow valve. I've truncated lists, and shortened things where I could, and placed the expanded versions in the Expansion Pack. Checklists and blueprint-styled worksheets are better delivered as nicely formatted PDF printables, instead of pages crammed in the back of a printed book. I've tried to make the Expansion Pack professional in appearance, so you can keep it on your desk, use it with your team at work, or show it to your boss. Feel free to use it in any way you want—you have my permission. Just be cool, cite your source as appropriate, and don't sell it.

Join Me on Instagram

I'd love to have you follow me on Instagram. You'll find me @mrjasonmiles. When you do, be sure to say hi. I'd be honored to follow you, too—maybe you've got a product I need? Maybe I'm your ideal prospect? Let's find out together on Instagram. Keep reading and let's see how quickly you can gather your tribe and unleash Instagram power in support of your online efforts.

P = PREP FOR SUCCESS

*If you have the courage to begin, you
have the courage to succeed.*

ZIG ZIGLAR
@thezigziglar on Instagram

Join Instagram and Get Your Business Profile

It's never too late for a new beginning in your life.

JOYCE MEYER
@joycemeyer on Instagram

Before we dive right in to the account setup details, let me share two brief paragraphs about the remarkable rise of Instagram. The founders' story is incredibly inspiring, and tens of thousands of marketers around the world are now benefiting from their genius. Who are these guys?

The Remarkable Rise of Instagram

On October 6, 2010, two Stanford classmates, Kevin Systrom and Mike Krieger, launched the Instagram app (Figure 1.1). They were backed by $500,000 in investor funding from famed Silicon Valley firms Baseline Ventures and Andreessen Horowitz. Their hope was to catch the wave of phone-based picture taking and sharing. Apple had made it fun and easy with the launch of the iPhone 3, and improved it in the summer of 2010 with the iPhone 4. Systrom and Krieger

Figure 1.1 The Instagram App

were betting on the death of point-and-shoot cameras and the rise of phone-based sharing. They guessed right.

Two months after launch, Instagram had a million users. By September 2011, less than a year after launch, Instagram passed 10 million users. In April 2012, Facebook purchased Instagram for a billion dollars, and the user growth continued its phenomenal pace. By February 2013 there were 100 million monthly active users. In December 2016 the Instagram team reported passing 600 million monthly active users. At the time that this book is being written, according to Statista, Instagram has over 1 billion monthly active users, and the site shows no sign of slowing down. It has become one of the most widely used social networks on the planet.

Brand-New to Instagram— Read This Before Signing Up

For the rest of this chapter, we'll cover the process for signing up for Instagram as well as marketing strategy and advice related to launching a professional profile. If you're brand-new to Instagram and haven't signed up yet, I recommend you read the whole chapter before creating an account. There is marketing strategy connected to your profile, so you'll want to understand it before you make an early mistake.

The main thing to remember is that Instagram is designed to be primarily managed from your phone, not from your computer. As with all new tools, there is a learning curve that you struggle through until you feel confident with it. Don't worry. You'll get past that, you can do this! If you're already familiar with Instagram, then use this chapter to fill in any gaps in your knowledge.

The Power of the Profile

Let's talk about the importance of the profile briefly, then we'll do a step-by-step walk-through of getting your account set up and getting it listed as a business profile. It's time to get you up and running on Instagram.

Have you ever visited someone's Instagram profile and been immediately impressed, or maybe unimpressed? The reason is simple. Your profile is the most important piece of real estate you can manage on Instagram—so it's the starting point of successful Instagram marketing. It needs to be powerful, focused, and professional.

Spend time thinking about your ideal prospects and the messages that will resonate with them at an emotional level—and those that won't. Create your profile with your prospects in mind. Sort it out at the start—and find the deep meaning that you can bring to the work. Just like an archer shooting an arrow, each aspect of your profile and every piece of content you share has the ability to hit the bull's-eye, fall short by a bit, or be dangerously off the mark. Refine your aim. How far off the mark?

INSTAGRAM'S FANTASTIC RESOURCES

Because Instagram is constantly adding new information and refining its functionality, I'd encourage you to visit several of its online sites including:

1. **Its excellent help resources.** Visit the general help content at http://help.instagram.com. You'll find useful information related to using Instagram with content for general use as well as resources for various users such as parents, businesses, brands, and law enforcement.

2. **Its press release site.** Instagram also does a great job of announcing new features. To read those announcements, you'll also want to regularly visit https://instagram-press.com.

3. **Its business blog and resources.** Instagram has done a terrific job of creating a user-friendly destination for business owners. It includes training, success stories, access to approved partners, and more. You'll want to bookmark this site and visit it regularly. It is the ultimate online resource for business owners and marketers. Find it at https://business.instagram.com (Figure 1.2).

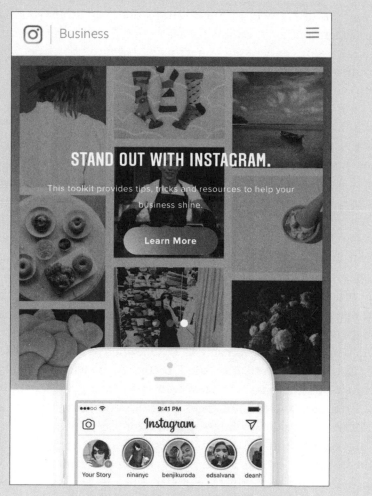

Figure 1.2 Instagram Business Resources

Power to Hurt Your Cause

If your profile is the most important piece of real estate you manage on Instagram, then it stands to reason that done poorly, your profile will hurt your chances of connecting with your tribe. A poorly done profile will be unclear and therefore unproductive. Worst case: it may even repel the very people you're trying to attract.

This shrink-sales-via-blunder scenario is actually a fairly well-documented situation in marketing work. To get a huge list of examples where media efforts backfired, simply google, "advertising that hurt sales." You'll find plenty of examples. I was surprised to see that Taco Bell's (@tacobell on Instagram) *Yo Quiero Taco Bell* campaign was on the list. It stuck in my mind as a fun idea, so I assumed it was successful—not so. Although it was a very popular phrase in the late nineties, and the cute little Chihuahua was good in the commercials—according to the company, tests proved that the campaign reduced sales by 6 percent. That was enough to get the CEO fired. The reason it didn't work? Many marketers believe it was because, although the message was memorable, it was ultimately a negative association. Dogs like Taco Bell food—so you should too? Maybe not.

The point is this: in each situation where a media effort damages sales, there is a clear reason it occurs. Although it is not obvious beforehand to the marketers involved, it becomes clear in time if they pay attention to their audience's behavior and learn along the way. This presents a doubly dangerous situation for your Instagram marketing because unlike TV commercials, you cannot easily test whether your Instagram profile is damaging your online efforts—or by how much. Don't make the mistake of just throwing spaghetti at the wall and hoping it sticks. Learn how to make and manage a professional Instagram profile that works well—it's a subtler art than you might at first appreciate, so invest the time to do it well.

A Powerful Profile Is Focused

On Instagram, you want your profile to quickly explain to visitors who you are, what you're all about, and what type of visual content they will get if they follow you. Professional. Clear. Customer focused. Never forget your profile is your Instagram home page—treat it with care.

If you're a thought leader or business coach, a profile that has authority and credibility is important. If you're a fashion blogger, then demonstrating your on-trend visual style is key. If you're a local Realtor, it might be social proof via houses sold or testimonials. Your profile lets existing customers as well as prospects know what you're using Instagram for and what they can expect. Prove to them that it will add value. As you can see in Figure 1.3, Whole Foods does a nice job of it (@wholefoods on Instagram).

Figure 1.3 Whole Foods

Profile Name Options

One of your most basic choices is the name you choose to use—whether to use a brand name, niche-related name, or your personal name. As with many marketing choices, there is no right or wrong. There is just a creative direction you get to decide upon, and then once you've decided, you get to live with it. Whatever you decide, it is important to make it crystal clear to current and prospective customers exactly who you are.

We'll dive more deeply into content strategy in the next chapter, but before we walk you through the account setup steps, let's cover niche selection. Of course, you can have more than one topic to discuss on your Instagram profile, but having clarity around it, especially if it's going to be connected to a username, is vital. A good starting point to help you figure out your Instagram niche is the Japanese concept of *ikigai*. This concept, which means "reason for being," focuses on four questions:

1. What do you love?

2. What are you good at?

3. What does the world (or your tribe) need?

4. What can you get paid for?

Take the time to consider these hard questions as you consider how to set up your Instagram profile and username and content strategy.

Don't be confused by the Instagram profile options. You'll notice that under the Edit Profile options, you have two name-related choices. First, your **Username**. This option governs your @username handle within the app, as well as the URL associated with your account when using a browser. So be careful when considering changing it. Change it and you change how people find you on Instagram. For example, if they search in the app or web-based tool, this is the name that will appear. The second option, simply titled **Name**, is the name displayed on your profile, just under your profile picture. Changing it doesn't alter how you're discovered or the URL associated with your account. That gives you some freedom to use it creatively. Consider it the place to include your slogan or tagline if you'd like.

The second profile challenge is selecting a name that isn't already taken. This is common to all the social sites, of course, and it can be a challenge for both business and personal profiles. In my case, there are several people named Jason Miles who are public figures trying to make their way in the world just like I am. One is an award-winning jazz musician, the other a country music singer. My profile name options are therefore limited. But on Instagram, we all lost out to a young name that was clearly an early adopter. He is "Jason Miles" on Instagram, and all the rest of us are something a little less clear. I chose to go with MrJasonMiles, so as to keep my name in the profile. Whatever you decide, try your best to maintain clarity and minimize confusion.

A NOTE ABOUT VERIFIED PROFILE BADGES

You may have noticed that some larger Instagram profiles have a blue badge with a checkmark in the middle next to the account name. While many people believe it's about the size of the following an account has received, it's not. It simply confirms that Instagram has verified the account for a public figure, celebrity, or global brand. In the past, there was no clear verification process, but as of summer 2018, there is now an automated request process. You can find the link to it in the mobile app under your Settings, then Request Verification.

The Powerful Profile Checklist

Let's work through the profile choices together in checklist format, then we'll walk you through the step-by-step setup process. Consider including as many of these elements as you can—some may be optional depending on whether you are setting up a business or personal profile. The more you can fit into the limited spaces available, the better. If you'd like a nicely formatted version of this checklist, be sure to visit www.winning.online and get our free Expansion Pack.

- [ ] A professional headshot or nicely formatted corporate logo. This doesn't have to be as formal as your LinkedIn profile picture, but you want to convey trustworthiness. Avoid the half-drunk selfies from your last excursion to Puerto Vallarta.
- [ ] A clear statement about who you are—and what you care about. If you're a company CEO or founder, be sure to include it. This explains a huge amount, as most people are very familiar with what Tim Ferris calls "job description as self-description."
- [ ] If it's a corporate/business account, include a clear statement about what your company does.
- [ ] A credibility indicator, an award, honor, or claim to fame. Position yourself for credibility but try not to sound like you're bragging.
- [ ] A description of the types of images you'll share. This can be hard to include in a 150-character bio.
- [ ] A link to other Instagram accounts you manage such as @sewpowerful in my case. These are clickable, so leverage this as much as possible. If you have both a personal and a corporate profile, be sure to cross-promote them.
- [ ] A link to your most appropriate website or content.
- [ ] Your business phone number, added in the business profile section of your profile.
- [ ] Your business email address, added in the business profile section of your profile.
- [ ] If you have an office or retail location, include the street address in your business profile, and a directions link will appear on your profile as well.
- [ ] The category your business operates in—this helps to define who you are nicely as well. You add this by selecting from a predetermined list of categories and subcategories in the business profile section.
- [ ] A call to action button—if there is one that fits your business situation. As with the category descriptor, you select this in the business profile section.
- [ ] A set of Story Highlights that answer top-of-mind visitor questions. Your Story Highlights can be used in really creative ways—take the time to consider how to add massive value to your ideal customers via this tool. In upcoming chapters we'll talk about creative ways to use your Story Highlights.

Don't Get Banned from Instagram

Mastering the functionality of Instagram isn't enough. We must also master a set of effective marketing techniques that result in good outcomes, while at the same time complying with Instagram policies. Unfortunately, there are a lot of shady marketers. Many of them trying to teach Instagram marketing, of course. Don't follow the advice of shady gurus. They may have gotten their prior results by breaking the rules—do your homework. Stay familiar with the helpful resources previously mentioned and do your homework on the following:

1. General Community Guidelines, many of which directly relate to how a marketer can and cannot behave on the site. If you want my three-word summary, it is "don't spam people."

2. Security Tips and Privacy information.

3. Guidelines written specifically for marketers related to using Instagram for business, including advertising on Instagram, linking accounts, and using branded content.

4. Terms related to what the company will do when your account is suspended or terminated.

5. The steps to take to close your account if you decide to no longer use the service.

6. The process for reporting abuse, copyright infringement, or your account being hacked.

There are specific things Instagram prohibits, and if you do them, you can get kicked off the platform. If that happens, Instagram prohibits you from joining again with a new account, so the price of violating these terms is very high. One example of a violation that seems tempting is to purchase an existing account to get started. That seems like it could be a great idea, but it violates Instagram's terms. So stay familiar with the terms and policies. You can find the full list under the Terms of Use statement. They include (condensed for our purposes):

1. You can't impersonate others or provide inaccurate information.

2. You can't do anything unlawful, misleading, or fraudulent.

3. You can't violate the terms or help or encourage others to violate them.

4. You can't do anything to impair the intended operation of Instagram.

5. You can't attempt to create accounts or collect information in unauthorized ways.

6. You can't attempt to buy, sell, or transfer any aspect of your account, or solicit, collect, or use login credentials or badges of other users.

7. You can't post private or confidential information or violate someone else's rights.

8. You can't use a domain name or URL in your username without Instagram's prior written consent.

Instagram Business Profiles and Tools Overview

Instagram's business profile feature allows you to change your standard user profile into a business profile—and subsequently gives you access to a wide variety of functions in support of business goals. Nonprofits and service organizations would also want to use this feature.

In the upcoming chapters of this book we'll discuss a wide variety of marketing strategies related to using Instagram's business tools, as well as marketing strategies designed to simply use the general Instagram features available to all users.

How to Get an Instagram Business Profile

Here are the steps involved in turning your personal profile into a business profile:

1. For iPhone users, from your profile tap the three horizontal bars in the top right corner. For Android users, in the top right corner you'll see three vertical dots to tap.

2. Select **Sign up for a business profile**.

3. Select **Convert Existing Account**.

4. Connecting your account to an existing Facebook page is optional, but to use the full functionality available, you'll need to do it.

5. Complete your business's contact information on the Set Up Your Business Profile page and select **Done**.

Find Your Heroes

One of the best ways to stay current and see the best practices as well as the trends is to simply make a set of model profiles that you check regularly. Find your heroes. Watch to see what other people in your niche or industry are doing—and learn from them. If you don't have any social media leaders within your niche or industry, then look beyond to public figures, celebrities, and national figures whom you respect and who have a strong social media marketing effort.

Now it's time to go deeper. In the next chapter, we'll dig into how to use the Instagram features. First we'll look at basic functionality, then we'll dive into two key parts of the platform, Instagram Stories and IGTV.

Mastering Basic Functionality

I fear not the man who has practiced 10,000 kicks once,
but I fear the man who has practiced one kick 10,000 times.

BRUCE LEE
@brucelee on Instagram, run by his daughter Shannon

Now that we've looked at the business profile options, let's look at general Instagram functionality. Some features are more complicated than others, but once you become familiar with them, you'll be up and running in no time. Although Instagram started as a photo sharing app, it has evolved way beyond just photos.

Three Ways to Publish

Instagram has three effective ways to publish content. It's important to have this mental framework so you understand how to learn, and then use, all the features. The three ways are the Feed, Stories, and IGTV:

Feed. This is the original photo and video sharing functionality. It's the oldest part of the matrix. Because of that, it is the best known and most used functionality. Instagram likes to refer to it simply as "Feed," but that's a little awkward, so in this book, you'll see me refer to it as "the Feed." The content is located on the Home tab, symbolized by the house in the bottom left corner of your primary navigation menu, so I'll also use "Home tab" to refer to it.

Stories. This is the ephemeral content (it goes away after 24 hours), although if you create a Story Highlight it remains permanently available. This was originally introduced to directly compete with Snapchat. It worked. Instagram has clearly won that war. People love Instagram Stories functionality. We'll do a deep dive into this functionality in Step 3.

IGTV. The newest publishing option focuses on sharing and watching vertical video. Is this Instagram's attempt at competing with YouTube? It would appear that way. Will it work? Time will tell.

Instagram General Functionality

For the rest of this chapter we'll work our way through the general functionality and the primary screens of Instagram. I'll mention Stories, Story Highlights, and IGTV when needed, but in the next chapter we'll explore those features more thoroughly since they play such a central role in the marketing efforts.

The five tabs of the primary navigation menu rest at the bottom of the screen almost constantly, so it is difficult to feel lost. Using the primary navigation menu as your constant frame of reference allows you to quickly navigate among the five screens. The only time the navigation menu is not at the bottom of the screen is when the Camera tab is in use, or when you're in Stories, IGTV, or on account setting, ad creation, or similar screens.

Let's explore each of the five major tabs to learn how they work and what they are designed to do. We'll look at them from left to right and from top to bottom. Remember, there are more extensive online tutorials and tips at http://help.instagram.com.

The Home Tab—Feed

Instagram continues to add functionality to the Home tab, aka Feed, in exciting ways (see Figure 2.1). The Home tab is in the bottom left corner of the screen and is designated by the house symbol.

Figure 2.1 Home Tab

The Home tab is the starting point for the following features:

Your Story Camera. The camera is accessed via the top left corner and symbolized by the camera icon. You can also simply swipe toward the right on your Home screen to access this feature. Content made via the Story Camera tool is designed to be used in the Stories feature. More on that in the next chapter.

IGTV. Accessible in the top middle right of the Home screen, IGTV is designed for watching long-form vertical video (formatted with your phone screen in mind). You can view IGTV content via both a stand-alone app available in the iTunes store and Google Play, or watch the content inside the main Instagram app. Videos can be between

15 seconds and 10 minutes for regular accounts, and larger and verified accounts can add videos up to an hour.

Direct messages. Access to your Instagram Direct messages (DMs) is available in the top right corner, symbolized by the arrow in the blue circle. Alternatively, you can simply swipe the Home screen toward the left to access this feature. Instagram refers to this as simply Instagram Direct, although most people refer to this functionality as DM-ing.

Video chat. You can also video chat an individual or up to four people via Instagram Direct. Simply select a profile you've DM'ed, or a group chat you've already set up, and in the top right corner you'll see a video camera icon. Tap it to place the video call. You can video chat for an unlimited amount of time.

Stories. The second section from the top on the Home screen displays stories—yours if you have any, as well as stories from people you follow. We'll devote a lot more detail to the use of story content in upcoming chapters.

Latest pictures. The lower section of the Home screen displays the latest pictures from the people you follow as well as advertisements. You scroll through these by swiping up. On the Home tab you can like and comment on these pictures quickly and easily. To like an image simply double tap it. In addition to showing the picture, the Home tab also shows the number of likes an image has received and the description entered by the author. As space allows, it will also show comments.

The Explore Tab

The Explore tab, shown in Figure 2.2 and accessed by tapping the magnifying glass icon, allows you to discover new Instagram users that you might like to follow and topics that are related to your industry or interests.

In older versions of Instagram, this was referred to as the Popular tab. It still functions in that manner. Let's talk about being popular on the Explore tab; then we'll discuss other ways you can use this tab effectively.

Figure 2.2 Explore Tab

Popular Images on the Explore Tab

Having an image displayed at the top of the Explore tab can boost your Instagram profile dramatically, allowing more people to learn about you quickly. Although Instagram doesn't reveal the exact methodology for getting an image into this enviable position, most people believe it is a combination of several factors. First, it's tailored to your unique use of the app, so everyone's Explore feed will look different. Blogger Chris Smith suggests that the factors include:

1. The number of likes you get from your followers within the first 10 to 20 minutes of posting the image.

2. The relative competition at the time. Each image is competing against other images in real time. As with any type

of popularity system, sometimes the competition is overly strong, and sometimes it happens to be weak.

3. The number of likes you receive from your followers compared with those from nonfollowers. Although people who find it by looking at a hashtag can like your image, it appears that more relative weight is given to likes that come from your followers.

Other Ways to Use the Explore Tab

Users can navigate the Explore tab by using the search bar, by categories, or simply by browsing popular images and videos. Let's review these options briefly.

First, you can tap in the search bar and begin looking for people, hashtags, or locations. Play with the search function to learn how it behaves and then adapt your efforts to optimize your outcome. If you want to find a personal or business profile, simply begin the search for specific users in the search bar, such as your own name or a business in your town. If you can't think of anyone, use "MrJasonMiles." Search for #JasonMiles and you'll find a whole bunch of Jason Mileses, most of whom aren't me. Again, the search algorithm will return results related to Username, Profile Name, Hashtags, and Locations, so consider carefully how to optimize your profile to include those elements!

Second, you can look at images by category. This allows you to narrow down your search for ideal content for such topics as Automotive, Humor, Music, Style, Sports, Fitness, Comics, Animals, Art, and more.

Third, you can search for specific hashtags, like #instagrampower. Don't worry; we'll discuss hashtags in much greater detail in Step 3. If you search for a hashtag, you'll see the images that have been tagged and the Instagram users who shared them. Following the Instagram users who regularly use hashtags related to your industry is probably a wise first step.

Fourth, you can search by places, geo-locating specific content. Want to see what images or videos are being shared from your neighborhood? Just search for it. Or maybe you want to see what is happening at Madison Square Garden—just search for it.

Fifth, you can simply browse the grid of pictures that Instagram provides to you. These users may or may not be of interest to you.

They are presented because they are popular, but that doesn't necessarily make them a good candidate for you to follow.

The Camera Tab

The Camera tab is located in the middle of the bottom of your screen, identified by the plus sign in the square. It provides an alternative method of accessing your phone's camera for posting an image or video. You can also access your phone's photo library. The video you record or share from the camera tab can be up to 60 seconds via this method. It adds the video to your Instagram Feed. Later in the chapter we'll talk about another way to create videos—through the Story functionality.

Ultimately, it is your choice about whether this method of accessing your phone's camera is useful to you or whether you use your phone's primary camera tool. The rationale for including this function in the Instagram app is that it allows you to go from picture taking to picture editing without ever leaving the app (see Figure 2.3).

In the Camera tab you can start by selecting an image from the Library, taking a photo, or recording a video. You can also turn the camera's flash on or off or allow it to be in auto-detect mode. Finally, you can switch between your phone's front camera and rear camera.

Once you either take a picture or choose an image from your image library, you will move to an editing screen. The Instagram editing screen allows you to conduct two primary activities. First, you can make edits to the image and put it into the final visual form you want to use. Second, you can prepare the written information that will accompany your image. Both of these activities are vitally important for marketing purposes. Social impact is a combination of imagery and messaging. Your ultimate success on Instagram will depend largely on the choices you make in these two categories. Let's take a closer look at each topic. Some of these topics will be the subject of later chapters in this book, so in those cases we'll briefly touch on the topic here.

Modifying Your Image

Instagram is about images, so it stands to reason that regardless of whatever else you want to accomplish by way of marketing goals, you also need to produce images that are very appealing to your ideal followers. That will be different in different niches and categories, but

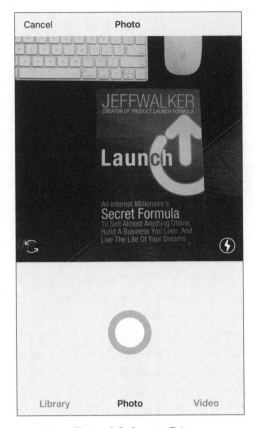

Figure 2.3 Camera Tab

the basics of professional photography must be mentioned. Let's walk through the options available for editing your images in the Camera tab section of Instagram:

Crop your image. There are three primary objectives when cropping an image. First, you want to narrow the focus and decide what element of the image should be the primary focal point. Second, you want to intentionally remove any unwanted elements from the image. Finally, you want to correct composition problems and align your image using the rule of thirds, which states that images are more interesting if placed off-center. The Instagram cropping feature automatically provides the grid that indicates the one-third lines. To resize the image simply use the pinch or pull function to make the image smaller or larger.

After you finalize the crop, you click **Next** to either add a filter or edit the image further. Your options include:

Filter options. In addition to simply keeping the image as is, referred to in filters as Normal, you can also select a range of effects from ultra-vibrant to black and white.

Edit options. After you finalize the filter decisions, you can select "Edit" to make additional changes, including adjusting the rotation, brightness, contrast, structure, warmth, saturation, color, fade, highlights, shadows, vignette effect, and tilt shift.

Caption and Metadata

You can add metadata to your images to help your followers learn more about the image. Metadata is information that accompanies your image but is not necessarily visible on the image. Preparing the metadata includes:

1. **Adding a caption.** Your description of the image is a vital part of communicating more details about the image. We will cover this in greater detail in Step 11. In addition to a description of the image and any call to action you'd like to include, you can also include hashtags. A hashtag is a categorization system originally pioneered on Twitter. It is simply a word proceeded by the # sign—for example, #sunset. This allows the image to be included in the category of images that have the #sunset hashtag. There are lots of terrific marketing activities that can be done with hashtags. We'll discuss them in more detail in Step 3.

2. **Tagging people.** You can include people in the photo. Simply click Tag People, tap the picture to identify the person you want to tag, and then search for them. You can repeat this step to tag multiple people. At the time that this book is being written there is not yet a way to tag people in a video.

3. **Adding location details.** Instagram identifies metadata on your image if it is available and attempts to offer you appropriate location options that you can quickly select. If you don't see the appropriate location name presented, you can type in a location.

4. **Social sharing.** If you connect them, you can allow your images and videos to be shared to Facebook, Twitter, and Tumblr.

5. **Advanced settings.** As we mentioned earlier, the advanced settings option allows creators to identify Branded Content. It also allows you to manage comments and enable the "Share Your Posts to Facebook" option to become a default setting.

The Activity Tab

The Activity tab, indicated by the heart icon, has three primary views (see Figure 2.4). The **You** view allows you to see the likes and comments that you've received most recently. It also allows you to view the results of any promotions you've run. It's a simple

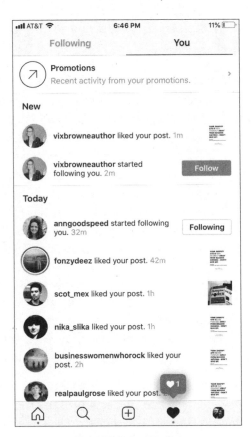

Figure 2.4 Activity Tab

way to keep up to date on what your followers are doing related to your images and account. The **Following** view summarizes the recent activity of the people you are following. This allows you to keep up on what other people are liking and commenting on. The **Promotions** view gives you access to your current advertising promotions.

The Profile Tab

The Profile tab is the final tab located on the far-right side of the bottom navigation menu. It is probably the most important tab for marketers. All the functions related to account management are accessed through this tab (see Figure 2.5). Let's review each Profile tab option starting at the top left corner.

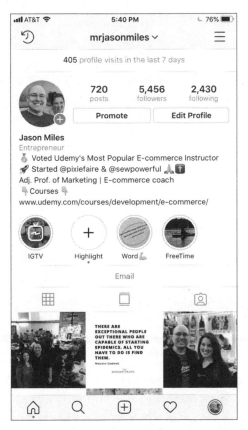

Figure 2.5 Profile Tab

Top left corner Story Archive icon. In the top left corner of the Profile tab you'll see the Story Archive—symbolized by a clock with an arrow around it. Tap it to reveal your archived story content. You can enable or disable your Story Archives in the Business Settings feature—more on those in a moment. The most common use is to create a Highlight. We'll talk about Highlights in upcoming chapters since they make a fantastic marketing opportunity. You can also simply take a story picture or video and publish it as a post.

Switch accounts. If you add a second account via the Business Settings (more on that in a moment), then you can switch between them by selecting the drop-down area next to your profile name in the middle of the top of the Profile screen. The second account you've added will be presented as an option. You can add more as needed. This allows you to switch between accounts without needing to log out and log in each time. See Figure 2.6.

Top right menu. In the top right corner of the Profile tab you'll see three vertical bars (Figure 2.7). Tap it to reveal a menu that includes Insights, Saved Content, Discover People, and Settings. Let's review each of these.

Insights. The Insights feature allows you to see your activity such as:

1. Interactions—actions taken on your account

2. Discovery—the accounts you've reached

3. Impressions—the number of accounts that have seen your content

4. Reach—the number of unique accounts that have seen any of your content

5. Profile Visits—the number of times your profile has been viewed

You can also view your content, including story insights and promotion results. If a promotion is not approved, you can access the appeal process as well. Finally, you can view your audience details including:

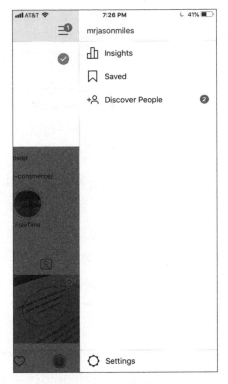

Figure 2.6 Switch Accounts in Profile Screen

Figure 2.7 Profile Menu

1. Top locations by city and country

2. Age range of your followers

3. The percentage of men versus women

4. The days of the week, and hour of the day, when your followers are most active

Saved Images/Collections. The Saved Images feature allows you to save an image and create collections of saved images. This is particularly useful when you want to create a collection of important Instagram accounts that you keep track of, such as an "Influencers" collection or a "Heroes" collection. Simply save an image from an account into a new collection you label "Influencers" and start adding to it. Over time, it will allow you to keep track of key accounts.

Discover People. The Discover People feature, symbolized by a person with a plus sign, allows you to discover new people either via your contacts or from Instagram suggestions.

Settings. The bottom right corner of the menu tab allows you to access your account settings by tapping the gear symbol. In Settings, you can do the following:

1. Find and invite friends.

2. View the photos you've liked.

3. Log out.

4. Modify your sharing settings, including how your account is connected to Facebook and other social media sites.

5. Manage your push notifications. Push notifications are emails you receive from Instagram when certain actions occur, such as when your images are liked or commented on.

6. Clear your search history.

7. Modify your privacy settings, including the option to require your approval before someone can follow you.

8. Manage how your photos are saved.

Managing Your Business Setting

Instagram's business tools are designed to give you both insight and expanded functionality as a marketer. I won't bore you by listing and describing each minor account setting option, but I'd encourage you to walk through the account management settings and explore each one. Let's walk through the major features.

Creating ads. We'll do a deep dive into advertising on Instagram in Step 14. Instagram ads can be made either within Instagram or via the Facebook Ads Manager—as long as you are an admin on the Facebook page connected to your Instagram business profile.

Set up Shoppable Posts function. For Instagram business account users that qualify, adding Shop buttons on posts allows viewers to simply tap on the screen to see a product image, price, and a link that goes to that item on your website. We'll cover this in detail in Step 12. This functionality is enabled by creating a Facebook Catalog and connecting it to your Instagram account. You can do this on your Facebook business page, or Shopify users and BigCommerce users can set this up directly on their websites, which is a fantastic feature.

Managing Branded Content. Instagram requires influencers to disclose when they are being compensated to share a product and to also identify the promotional partner. Influencer marketing is one of the hottest marketing developments in recent years, and it works really well on Instagram. We will focus on exactly how to do this in Step 16, and then show you how to become an influencer in Step 17.

To help influencers manage disclosure properly, Instagram created the Branded Content feature. It is available to Creators and Publishers. When it is used by the content publisher, the post or story they share will display "**Paid partnership with** . . ." above the post. If you're a content creator or an influencer and want to learn more about this feature and how to enable it, be sure to visit http://help .instagram.com and look in the Instagram for Business section and then read the Branded Content on Instagram information.

Adding a Call-To-Action to your profile. Your business profile already allows you to add a Call-To-Action so people can call you, text you, get directions, and email you. Tiffany Jewelers (@tiffanyandco on Instagram) does a nice job of this (Figure 2.8). Instagram is rolling out new functionality along these lines, so stay tuned. As of this writing, you can also enable book an appointment, buy tickets, place an order, shop (if you have the Shoppable Posts functionality approved and set up), and make a reservation. These are made possible via third-party apps. To see what is available, go to your business profile and select **Edit Profile**. In the business information section, click **Add an action button**. Then in the Business information section, select **Contact Options**, then **Add an action button**. You'll see the full list

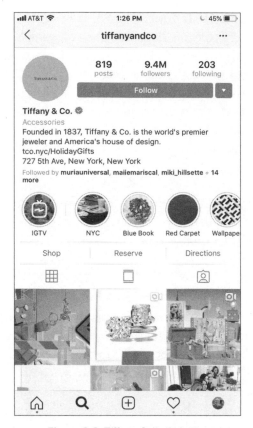

Figure 2.8 Tiffany Calls to Action

of third-party services on the screen. To enable the functionality, you must register as a user with the third-party service you want to use, then select it on Instagram and complete the setup process.

Activity status. In the second row you'll see a note that says, "[number] profile visits in the last 7 days." Tap this number and you'll be taken to your insights data.

Account stats. Just below the Activity Status, you'll see the number of posts you've added, the number of followers you have, and the number of accounts you've followed. These are all active links, so you can tap them and see the details.

Promote Button. The Promote Button allows you to set up a promotion quickly and easily in support of any of your published content. If your account is connected to Facebook, and you have a credit card on file, then the payment options will show it.

Edit Profile. The Edit Profile button allows you to change your profile information, including:

1. Profile photo

2. Username

3. Website

4. Bio (up to 150 characters)

5. Business information, including Facebook page, category, and contact information

6. Private information, including email, phone, and gender

Story Highlights. Below your profile information you'll see your Story Highlights section. We'll explore how to set up this feature in the next chapter.

Email and Directions. When viewing a business account, just below the Story Highlights, you'll see the option to access either the email or driving directions if the company has entered those in its profile.

Grid, Recent, or Mentions. Just above the pictures you've added you'll see a viewing option that allows you to see images in a grid view or individually, or to see photos where the account profile has been mentioned. When viewing your own profile, you can also see photos you've saved.

The Website Version of Your Instagram Profile

You can also view your Instagram profile on your computer, although the functionality is very limited. The domain name structure simply

Figure 2.9 Website Version of Instagram Profile

places the Instagram user name at the end of the URL—for example, http://www.instagram.com/sewpowerful, as shown in Figure 2.9.

The most common use of the web version is to use it as the destination for any Instagram social buttons on your website. In that way, visitors looking at your website from a computer can click on the Instagram social icon and see your Instagram profile on their screen, and follow you. Then when they are on their phone and open Instagram, they'll have made that connection. In the upcoming chapters we'll also look at methods for using your own, and other people's, Instagram images on your website.

Now that you know how to set up a profile and understand the basics of Instagram business accounts, it's time to go deeper. In the next chapter, we'll learn how to use the functionality for both Instagram Stories and IGTV. These two publishing options are exciting aspects of the Instagram platform.

SNAPSHOT

1. Take the time to learn about the Instagram tabs and how they work.

2. Explore the business profile settings.

3. Use the Explore tab to find people in your niche or industry to follow.

4. Start to consider how your profile image and description can effectively represent your work on Instagram.

Mastering Instagram Stories and IGTV

Marketing is telling a story about your value that resonates with enough people that they want to give you money.

SETH GODIN
@sethgodin on Instagram

Now that we've looked at basic account setup, let's dive deeper into two substantial Instagram features—Stories and IGTV. In this chapter, we'll simply discuss the functionality so you know how to access and use the features. Then, in upcoming chapters, we'll focus on learning how to create interesting marketing campaigns utilizing these features to grow your tribe.

Instagram Stories Overview

Instagram Stories launched on August 2, 2016. Although Instagram has allowed video sharing for a long time, the addition of Stories transformed it into a much more creative video publishing and viewing platform designed to directly compete with a key rival, Snapchat. Whole Foods (@wholefoods on Instagram) does a nice job of using Stories (Figure 3.1).

Figure 3.1 Whole Foods Story

What's Ephemeral Content?

Stories brought the concept of ephemeral content to Instagram. *Ephemeral* means the content lasts for only a limited time (24 hours) before it is no longer visible on the site. To create a bridge between the ephemeral content and the permanent content, Instagram created Story Highlights, a very cool feature that allows content creators to save story content in a nice way (more on how to leverage this concept in the next chapter). Snapchat popularized the concept of ephemeral marketing and was an up-and-coming rocket ship until Instagram launched Stories.

When Instagram launched Stories, it was widely seen as a "copy what is working" strategy. By the summer of 2018 Instagram announced that Stories had over 400 million daily active users, up from 250 million in 2017. That makes it twice as popular as Snapchat, which reportedly had just 190 million daily active users for the same time period.

Viewing Stories

While they're live, you can access your story content and the stories of people you follow in two ways. First, on the Home tab, you can see stories featured in the top section of the screen. Second, on the Profile tab, you can simply tap your account profile picture to see your own stories. While looking at stories you can:

See Viewers. Tap "Seen by . . ." in the bottom left corner to see who has viewed the content and also insights related to engagement.

Add to Highlights. This allows you to transfer the story to your Story Highlights.

More. Tap "More" in the bottom right corner. This option allows you to delete the content, save the content, send it to someone, or access your Story Settings.

What Can You Do with Stories?

The Stories functionality includes a nice set of publishing options. These radically expanded the functionality of Instagram when they were launched in 2016. You can use Stories to create:

- Instagram Story Photo(s) (exist for only 24 hours)

- Instagram Story Boomerang Videos (1 second) (exists for only 24 hours)

- Instagram Story Video (up to 15 seconds) (exists for only 24 hours)

- Instagram Story Highlight (preserves story content and strings it together)

Accessing Your Story Camera

You can access your Story Camera in two ways. First, via the top left corner of your Home tab (Figure 3.2). It is symbolized by the camera icon. You can also simply swipe toward the right on your Home tab to access the camera.

Using Your Story Camera Functionality

Let's review the Stories functionality from top to bottom and left to right (Figure 3.3).

Story Settings. The gear icon in the top left corner gives you access to your Story Settings. Options include:

- Hiding your story

- Allowing replies

- Allowing sharing

Figure 3.2 Story Camera Icon (upper left)

Figure 3.3 Stories Functions

- Saving to Camera Roll

- Saving to Archive

- Sharing your story to Facebook

- Allowing Highlights resharing

Exit Story Camera. You can exit the Story Camera by tapping the arrow in the top right corner. This returns you to your Home tab.

Camera Roll. Access your camera's photos by tapping the small photo displayed in the bottom left of the Story Camera screen.

Camera flash settings. Toggle through your camera's flash settings by tapping the lightning bolt icon.

Camera button. Take a picture by tapping the camera button (circle) in the middle of the screen, or record a 15-second video by holding it down.

Under the camera button you have a set of slider options including:

- **Type.** Gives you a blank screen to write something on.

- **Live.** Allows you to begin an Instagram Live video. These can be up to one hour in length.

- **Normal.** Allows you to operate your camera.

- **Boomerang.** Allows you to record 1-second video clips.

- **Focus.** Allows you to use your camera's depth of field, if you have an iPhone 8+ or 10.

- **Superzoom.** Allows you to add fun effects to a brief video clip.

- **Rewind.** Allows you to record a brief video that is played in reverse.

- **Hands Free.** After you tap record, the video will continue to record for 15 seconds.

Front/Back Camera. Switch between your phone's front and back camera by tapping the two arrows.

Add Graphics. Tap the smiley face in the bottom left corner to access graphics to add to your content.

After you add your content, you'll be given an editing screen with menu options along the top of the photo. They include

Link IGTV. Add a link to an IGTV video.

Add Stickers. Stickers include:

- **A music sticker.** These allow you to add a song.
- **A poll sticker or emoji slider sticker.** These allow you to write your own question. After it's published, followers can vote and see the real-time results.
- **Location sticker.** Search by location and add it to your content.
- **Hashtag sticker.** These allow viewers to see a hashtag you add and tap it to see all the content associated with that hashtag.

Volume on/off. This removes the volume from video clips if you prefer.

Drawing tool. Write freehand, draw, or highlight things on your content.

Typing tool. Add a typed message on your content.

Story Highlights

By creating a Story Highlight, you can make story content permanently available. You can also create interesting mash-ups of story content in a strategic way to orient and educate your profile visitors.

Create a Story Highlight. While looking at any one of your story posts that are still public, or your Story Archive with prior story content you've published, click the Highlight option at the bottom of the screen. You'll be prompted to either add it to an existing Story

Figure 3.4 Add to Highlights

Highlight or to create a new one (Figure 3.4). Story Highlights are displayed on your Profile tab.

Edit your Story Highlight. You can edit any Story Highlight by viewing it and tapping "More" in the bottom right corner of the screen. You can do the following:

- Change the name of the Story Highlight.

- Change the cover image of the Story Highlight. (This is an opportunity to be visually creative.)

- Send it to a contact.

- Copy the Story Highlight link. This allows you to use it in creative ways off Instagram.

What Is IGTV, and How Do You Get It Set Up?

On June 20, 2018, Instagram launched Instagram TV (IGTV) for viewing and sharing vertical (aka portrait orientation) videos. While you can download the stand-alone IGTV app, you can also view all the IGTV content within the existing Instagram app, so all Instagram users have immediate access, which was a smart move. You can download the IGTV app for iPhone in the App Store, or for Android in Google Play (Figure 3.5).

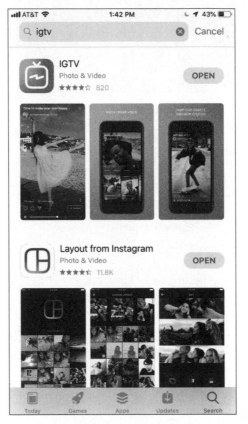

Figure 3.5 IGTV App

The IGTV Video Specs

- **Video format:** MP4.

- **Aspect ratio:** Minimum 4:5 up to a maximum of 9:16.

- **Length:** Smaller accounts, 15 seconds to 10 minutes. Larger verified accounts, 15 seconds to 60 minutes.

- **Orientation:** Vertical (aka portrait).

- **Size:** 650 MB for videos less than 10 minutes and 3.6 GB for videos up to 60 minutes.

- **Videos should have a minimum rate of 30 frames** per second, and a minimum resolution of 720 pixels.

How Do I Create an IGTV Channel?

From the Instagram app, tap the TV icon in the top right corner of the Home tab, or download the IGTV app from the App Store or Google Play. Then tap the gear for settings and "Create Channel" and follow the prompts. From your computer you can visit www.instagram.com and go to your profile and tap or click IGTV. Click "Get Started" and follow the on-screen prompts.

How Do I Add Videos to IGTV?

From the Instagram App or IGTV App. To add video to IGTV from Instagram, browse to IGTV from your Home tab and view your channel by tapping on your profile picture. Then tap the plus sign (+) to select a video. Add a cover photo, title, and description. Click "Post."

From Your Computer. Browse to your Instagram account, www .instagram.com/[username]. Click "IGTV," then "Upload." Click the plus sign to add a video or drag and drop it. Add a cover photo, title, and description. (See Figure 3.6.)

Figure 3.6 Adding an IGTV Video

Which Format Should I Shoot In?

The biggest challenge we face as marketers is to decide which format to shoot in. The only right answer is to decide where you want the content to be shown, and then plan accordingly. Vertical video has traditionally been done for shorter content pieces of just a few minutes, while horizontal video has traditionally been used for longer content. Time will tell whether that stays true or not.

Since IGTV requires videos to be vertical and YouTube and Facebook both now automatically detect and adapt to the vertical format for their viewers in their mobile apps, it seems clear the transition to vertical video is well underway. In fact, Mashable declared 2017 "the year video went vertical." This makes sense—as more video consumption is done on smartphones, smart marketers will optimize their work for that format.

As a marketer, that means you can shoot in vertical mode on your phone and it will be displayed well on all of these mobile platforms. It's not seen as "wrong" or a rookie mistake anymore. That's great news. Chances are, the desktop versions are all going to start displaying these videos nicely as well, meaning without the black bars on the left and right side of the video.

The downside to this change? Well, there are three obvious issues. You'll have to decide how best to navigate these new waters. Here are the challenges.

First, now you've got to think about your video creation work with two forms in mind. Landscape orientation will still be optimal for computer screens and TV viewing, while vertical will be optimal for smartphones and tablets. If you work with videographers or agencies, you'll have to clarify your intended use—and they'll have to adjust accordingly.

Second, the style of video creation for vertical is different than for horizontal. You have to consider your surroundings and how the physical environment you interact with will be displayed. In general, vertical video has long been associated with short, candid, personally recorded videos from your smartphone. The production value was lower than horizontal videos. Will that continue? I guess time will tell.

Third, all your old video content is likely shot in a landscape orientation. You may have paid a huge amount of money to have that content created, and unfortunately, you can't upload any of it to IGTV as it currently exists. So, you'll have to have it edited to a vertical form. When you do that, you can actually add a little bit of creative copywriting above and below the video. This is true for both Stories and IGTV. See Figure 3.7 for an example from a story.

Figure 3.7 Creative Copywriting with Content Edited to Vertical

Uploading Horizontal Videos to IGTV Anyhow

Instagram wants you to upload vertical video. But lots of your professionally done video is going to be horizontal. So you can always simply edit the video in your video editing software, rotating the dimensions and rendering it to play in portrait orientation. Your aspect ratio must be 4:5 to 9:16, but you can still save a file with those dimensions simply reversed, upload it, and have it play sideways, which viewers will then interpret to mean "turn your phone sideways." For example, GaryVee uploads his horizontal videos to IGTV as vertical video and even has a brief "Rotate Your Phone" call to action at the beginning of the video (Figure 3.8).

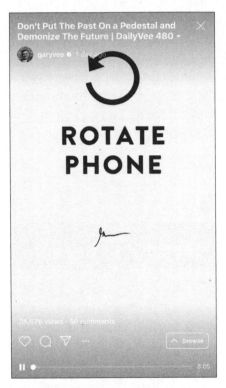

Now that you know how to set up a profile and understand the basics of Instagram business accounts, it's time to transition into an emphasis on finding and attracting your tribe. In the next chapter, we'll learn how to use hashtags to do this. Then we'll start adding marketing strategies.

Figure 3.8 Horizontal Video with "Rotate Phone" Message

SNAPSHOT

1. Take the time to learn how both Instagram Stories and IGTV work.

2. Look at your website version, http://www.instagram.com /[your user profile name], to see how your images look on a desktop computer.

3. See how the people you are following use Stories and IGTV and begin learning from them.

4. Start to consider what types of content will best represent your business.

Master Hashtags

I like hashtags because they look like waffles.

UNKNOWN

According to Instagram, over 95 million pieces of content are shared on the platform each day. How do you keep track of all that information? Hashtags have become our best hope—and Instagram uses them really well. If a librarian like old Melvil Dewey, creator of the Dewey Decimal Classification system, was around today, he'd give hashtags a thumbs-up and a happy-face emoji wink wink.

Where Did Hashtags Come From?

Twitter user Chris Messina created the concept of using the hashtag for social media conversations. On August 23, 2007, he tweeted a suggestion to use the # sign before the keyword or phrase as a method of categorizing conversations within the site. His innovation didn't gain widespread acceptance immediately. People complained that including # signs made messages difficult to read.

The system gained real social acceptance later that year during the San Diego wildfires. The hashtag #sandiegofire became the organizing phrase that enabled people to communicate quickly and conveniently on the site. The method of using the # sign in front of a word or phrase, although distracting to people reading the message, proved very useful.

Twitter coined the name *hashtag*, and on July 1, 2009, the company began hyperlinking the hashtagged words together in search results, making the function of using hashtags very convenient. The list of social networks and related sites that have adopted this practice is fairly extensive.

How Instagram Uses Hashtags

So how do hashtags work on Instagram? When you share content on Instagram and include a hashtag in the caption, anyone can tap that hashtag and see other images that have used it too. The content is displayed via the Explore tab with three useful options. See Figure 4.1.

1. **Related hashtags.** As the name implies, this displays similar hashtags that may be of interest. There aren't related hashtags for every hashtag, but for the more popular hashtags there are and it can be a useful way to identify similar user groups within a topic or industry.

2. **The Top view.** This view displays content that has the most engagement—the most likes and comments. The nice part about this feature is that the cream rises to the top. So if you're trying to make yourself known using a specific hashtag and your content happens to be well liked, then viewers of that hashtag will likely see it, even long after you've shared the content. For example, when looking at the top content for #instagrampower, you can still see posts that came out during the initial book launch for the first edition in 2013 by scrolling down the feed just a bit, even though it's been used over 1,500 times.

3. **The Recent view.** As its name implies, this view shares the content with the most recent use of the hashtag at the top of the feed. For less popular hashtags, the most recent images will be visible toward the top for longer. For more popular hashtags, you'll have to scroll farther down the feed to find them.

Figure 4.1 Hashtags in Explore

MARKETING STRATEGY TIP—HASHTAGS YOU CAN "TRY" TO CONTROL

If you include a very popular hashtag with your content, it will likely be shown at the top of the Recent feed for just a split second, and it will also be very hard to get ranked in the Top view for that hashtag. But if you include a less popular hashtag, it will stay on the top of the Recent feed for a longer period of time. It will also be much easier to get it to rank in the Top view. The sweet spot is somewhere in the middle—hashtags that are used in your niche, but not so popular as to be hard to influence and impossible to be a leader in.

How to Use Hashtags

Hashtags have enormous utility for creative marketers. Let's review a few of the powerful ways you can leverage them.

1. Include them on your posts to expand the reach of the content. You can include up to 30, but that is probably a little excessive.

2. You can create your own hashtags and use them creatively in your business for things like contests, promotions, and thought leadership.

3. You can look for hashtags, and now you can follow them as well, to research popular trends and participate in conversations within your industry or niche by commenting, liking, or sharing your own content using that hashtag.

4. You can identify new prospects by looking to see who is using relevant hashtags.

Create Your Own Hashtags

Creating your own hashtags enables a nice collection of marketing activities, including leading conversations and creating topics that rally customers and interested prospects in ad hoc conversations and sharing. Being the thought leader also positions you as the leader of your tribe. Creating a hashtag for a specific customer purpose also gives you the opportunity to ask people to use that custom hashtag as a social media reply device. This approach is what powers most Instagram contests, which we'll cover more deeply in Step 11.

Hashtags can be set up by anyone simply using the # symbol before a word or phrase. You can use any hashtag you'd like without needing anyone's permission. That's good news for creative types, but an obvious problem occurs—hashtag wars! When two dueling marketers try to use a hashtag for different purposes, things can get confusing. Hashtags can also be used in association with negative or inappropriate images, so practice care.

As a marketer, there are some best practices that you need to keep in mind when you start to consider how best to create and utilize hashtags. Let's review them:

1. Be brief—use either one word or a short phrase.

2. Try to create a hashtag that is memorable and easily understood.

3. Check to make sure the hashtag is not open to multiple interpretations, or else it runs the risk of being used for the wrong purpose. Be careful here, weird things can happen.

4. Check to make sure the hashtag is not already in use before creating it. Make your hashtags unique or they'll be used by others and therefore become more problematic as people use them for random things.

5. Don't create hashtags that include another company's brand or product name, except for rare occasions, like this book— please take a picture and share it using the #instagrampower and #instagrampowerbook hashtags.

6. Remember that once you set up a hashtag, it becomes a communication tool for anyone to use. What you popularize, others can hijack. You cannot control its use.

Research Trends in Your Niche

Even in a tiny niche, like the doll clothes market, there are new topics, trends, and concepts being created all the time. New competitors come into the market, new events happen, and industry news comes and goes. By following thought leaders in your industry and watching their use of hashtags, you can quickly keep your finger on the pulse of trending topics. Because of the visual nature of Instagram, this type of research is even more helpful for product sellers because you can get a quick look at new items you might not otherwise see.

Save and Cut and Paste

Search for terms through Instagram's Explore tab until you discover what your niche's customers are commonly using. Then consider making a list of the hashtags on your phone's notes function so you can easily cut and paste them into your Instagram caption each time they are needed.

Find Prospects Using Hashtags

You have an opportunity to identify people who are interested in your niche or industry. Simply look to see who is sharing pictures using the related hashtags. This is a significant opportunity that is easy to do. You can also follow a hashtag. When you do that, you see the items shared that use the hashtag and you can quickly like and comment on the content.

The Great Placement Debate

In the early days of Instagram people were sensitive to not use more than a couple of hashtags, and they would frequently only place them in the first comment, rather than in the caption. Those practices have shifted. Now people use tons of hashtags, and they also include them in the caption. To make the caption statement stand out and not be crammed into one giant paragraph with a lot of hashtags, users often add a space or two under their comment, include a period or two, and then add all their hashtags. That separates them nicely from your written comments.

Join in the Sharing

In some industries or niches, using the common hashtags can feel like a giant waste of time, and it might be. But in other niches, participating in the trending topics is a simple way to engage with prospective customers. You'll have to decide whether this is a good approach for your situation.

One indicator of whether your time will be well spent joining a conversation via a hashtag or using it for an Instagram image is whether you are (or your brand is) fairly well known and respected. If so, then you have an easy way to make a strong social impact. If not, then you'll need to work much harder to make yourself known, and you'll have to determine if that is time well spent. If you are a product marketer, the answer is probably a strong yes. If you are a service provider, then you'll likely want to focus on local hashtags to connect with local prospects. As with all other forms of advertising, you probably need to take a long-term view and not make up your mind based on one or two attempts.

Cautionary Tales

As mentioned previously, companies have learned that hashtags can be hijacked and used for customer complaints. Hashtags are wild and free. Once created, they take on a power of their own. Creating a hashtag associated with your brand is the equivalent of setting up "open mic night" on the Internet. Be afraid, be very afraid. Setting up a popular hashtag and giving it prominence through your other media channels, only to have it constantly used to trash your company, is a PR nightmare. Be careful to consider your brand's reputation in the marketplace and whether it might be wiser to simply participate in industry conversations rather than creating unique hashtags that can be used against you.

McDonald's and the #McDStories Hashtag

McDonald's learned this the hard way when it set up a Twitter hashtag campaign. The initial hashtag it created was #MeetTheFarmers, which the company used effectively to share stories of healthy produce and locally sourced ingredients. McDonald's paid to promote the hashtag, so it gained wide prominence. A solid effort—no problems so far. But the second hashtag, #McDStories, was much more problematic.

Soon the hashtag was being used to share food poisoning stories, broadcast customer service complaints, mock the company with funny insults, and generally bash the brand. The anti-McDonald's sentiment turned into a competitive sport. Twitter users took turns coming up with the most sarcastic tweets they could, and happily tacked on the #McDStories hashtag to broadcast their messages.

The initial error was only one layer of the ordeal. Social media bloggers also took the opportunity to publicly correct the company on its approach. Not only did McDonald's receive mockery from the public; it received public criticism from social media marketers, too.

There are plenty of lessons to learn from the McDonald's story. Let's review them briefly:

1. A hashtag is a communication tool, and like any good tool, it can be used to build up or tear down. Hashtags are like a megaphone, and if you create one, it has power. If you take it a step further and advertise it on your other media channels, you give it even more prominence and power.

2. Crafting hashtags in a focused way that shapes the conversation in a direction of your choosing is wiser than making them more general. The #MeetTheFarmers hashtag didn't provide an easy on-ramp to complaints like the #McDStories hashtag did.

3. Your brand resides in the mind of the consumer. If you ask people to share their thoughts publicly, you might be surprised at the level of negativity. Don't expect them to be "on message." In social media, this inability to control the message is particularly problematic for larger brands that have negative consumer sentiment to deal with. It doesn't mean they shouldn't use social media; it means they should be careful how they structure the engagement.

Hashtag Dos and Don'ts

We hope these cautionary tales have helped clarify the importance of getting your plan nailed down when it comes to using hashtags. Let's review a list of best practices.

Hashtag Dos

1. Do take the time to research the hashtags associated with your industry and learn how they are best used.

2. Do participate in the use of hashtags to extend your message to a broad audience.

3. Do look to see who is using your niche or industry hashtags and follow them.

4. Do use caution when creating new hashtags to ensure you can shape the dialogue as much as possible.

5. Do create hashtags that are brief and easily understood.

6. Do use websites that help you learn about new hashtags and keep up on trending topics.

Hashtag Don'ts

1. Don't forget that hashtags are a tool that can be used to do damage.

2. Don't underestimate the negative sentiment that might be bottled up about your brand and unleashed via hashtags.

3. Don't create hashtags that are too general and open to broad interpretation or multiple meanings.

4. Don't use general trending hashtags for marketing purposes.

5. Don't create hashtags with brand names that you do not have express permission to manage.

6. Don't overuse hashtags. Most people suggest using between 2 and 10, but no more. Technically you can add up to 30, but that is not recommended unless you've really considered the impact. Adding a long list of hashtags could make you look a little too desperate.

An Interview with a Hashtag Pioneer—Josh Decker

One of the most creative uses of hashtags I've ever seen is at professional sporting events. For example, at Seattle Mariners games, where the fan content was shared on the jumbotrons in near real-time as they posted using hashtags. Have you seen that at events you've attended? When I first saw it, I was blown away by the beauty of the idea—turning fans into the stars of the show. It's one of my family's favorite parts of the day! See Figure 4.2.

Figure 4.2 Fan Content Shared on a Jumbotron

The company behind the technology is Seattle-based Tagboard, founded by Josh Decker. Tagboard partners with more than 200 major sports teams, and its technology is used at the largest events around the world. Tagboard also powers on-air sharing of social content for TV broadcasts. I asked Josh to share more about his journey and his perspective on hashtags:

Q: How did you come up with the idea for Tagboard?

A: The idea for Tagboard came about because communities all over the world were using digital communication channels, but those conversations were disconnected. We wanted to connect these people. We wanted it to work across social networks and be opt-in. The hashtag became a way for people to connect. When I had the idea for Tagboard, it was 2010—you should have heard me trying to explain this idea to my mom. She thought I was crazy. But we thought, *Hey, we think this hashtag thing will catch on and spread, and we'll have something pretty awesome to work with.* And that's the idea of what you see at a Mariners game. You use that hashtag and you get added to the pool of content that the Mariners team can choose to put up onscreen. It's a way for the fan to get rewarded for communicating and connecting with the community.

Q: Was there a specific breakthrough moment when you realized this was going to be a commercially successful idea and that hashtags were going to power the idea?

A: It was the first time I saw a hashtag used in a commercial on TV. I'm an Audi guy. I had the idea for Tagboard because I was part of an Audi community and wanted to improve the way we communicated online. Audi, being a very digitally savvy brand, had the first commercial with a hashtag. It was a Super Bowl commercial in 2011, and I thought, *Oh snap! We're going mainstream.* This was around the same time we launched the company. We'd been working on it for six months, but when I saw that hashtag, I knew we were on the right track.

Q: Is Tagboard just for big brands, or can smaller businesses use it too? What are some use cases that our audience might be surprised to read about?

A: Tagboard, when we started, was not supposed to be a software-as-a-service company. It was a user-focused tool. It was more about helping anyone connect with their community online. We didn't get traction on the user side, but brands and marketers saw the value in it. We've proudly kept a free search option on our website that anyone can use. We've had over 5 million hashtags searched on our website.

The great thing is that we're able to work with the NBA Finals, or World Cup, but we believe that it should be accessible to anyone. We have large enterprise-level solutions, but we also have our free search tool, so we're able to serve anyone.

Q: At a social/cultural level, what do you think the highest and best use of Tagboard and hashtags is?

A: I continue to be blown away when Tagboard is used to not only share breaking news, but to connect the people who are affected by that news. I've seen it used for earthquakes, wildfires, building fires, crane collapses, and shootings that are becoming way too common. Any time a big event happens, news networks are using Tagboard to break the story, because Tagboard is the only way to help them access that breaking news content, live from the scene, in real time, on any social network, giving them the ability to find that content and use it to tell the news and share updates and alerts from the government or other official sources.

Q: How have you seen the commercial use of hashtags change since 2011?

A: Hashtags started as a way to thread conversations, and we lost that at some point, but now I feel like we've gone from this attitude of "Who can come up with the cutest hashtag" to more of a foundational component of a marketing campaign. It's cleaner, it's to-the-point, and it's more broadly used as a tactic to maintain consistency and relevance. You're not seeing as much of the noise around hashtags, and we're starting to see the signal come through. We're seeing hashtags used for more longer-run evergreen campaigns. Hashtags have gone back to the community. It started there, and then marketers got ahold of it, and overdid it, and it became a marketing thing, and we're seeing it shift back to a community orientation, even in the way marketers use them.

Q: Are there any tips or suggestions for readers that are trying to effectively use hashtags in support of their online work?

A: Listen to your community. If you're trying to come up with a new hashtag for your campaign? Don't. All you have to do is go online and see what your community is already using. Ninety percent of the time, the best way to come up with your hashtag is to listen to your audience. If you need to come up with your own, keep it short and simple.

Q: How about any cautions, warnings, or things to watch out for?

A: I'm always a fan of camel casing—capitalizing the first letter of a new word within the hashtag—because sometimes you can miss some double meanings that won't show up otherwise. And don't overdo it. Don't force it. Communities are built on trust, and when they feel like you're forcing something down their throat, they won't trust you. At the end of the day, you can't force it.

Q: If readers want to learn more about using Tagboard, what should they do?

A: Check out our website, tagboard.com, or scroll through our Twitter feed @Tagboard. We share a lot of the work our clients do on Twitter, so you can get a great taste for how the product works, and how it's used in the real world.

SNAPSHOT

1. Hashtags are a great tool for engaging with customers.

2. Include them with your content as you share it.

3. Use hashtags to research your industry and connect with new prospects.

4. Remember that if you create a hashtag in association with your brand, anyone can use it, including haters.

A Side Step for Nonprofits, Local Marketers, and Service Providers

Instagram can work well for nonprofits, local marketers, and service providers. Why? Because your tribe is there—just waiting to rally in support of your efforts. If your work can be shared visually, either in photo or video form, then you can leverage the Instagram platform regardless of whether you have physical items to sell or not. In this chapter, we'll dive into the options for each of these types of Instagram users and share success stories for inspiration.

Nonprofit Marketing on Instagram

Charities have plenty of ways to leverage the power of Instagram. My wife and I run a nonprofit, and you can see our work on Instagram @sewpowerful. One nonprofit we look up to and see as an inspiration on Instagram is Charity:water. It has more than 385,000 Instagram followers at the time of this writing and an incredibly compelling Instagram profile. Charity:water is using the platform brilliantly. See its work @charitywater.

Figure 5.1 Charity:Water on Instagram

The most difficult challenge many nonprofits face is finding prospective donors who care about the cause. Some charities have it easier than others. But every nonprofit marketing manager must ask how the basic mission of the organization can be presented in a visually compelling way. The initial goal in nonprofit marketing is capturing people's attention. A compelling picture or video has the power to do that in remarkable ways (see Figure 5.1). Adding a quote to a picture compounds the potential impact and shapes the prospect's thinking.

Local Marketing with Instagram

Local marketing via Instagram is a hot topic. (See Figure 5.2.) And the good news is that the tools and techniques for integrating rich media into your local marketing efforts have never been better.

Figure 5.2 Pike Place Public Market

The Old Way vs. the New Way

The period of affinity-based social media was really from 2004 to 2010. The large-scale platforms that connected people according to their similarities were the "killer apps" of the Web 2.0 movement. Myspace, Facebook, YouTube, Twitter—each of these sites was envisioned as an affinity- or function-based approach without deliberate emphasis on strengthening local connections. They weren't bad for local marketers, but they weren't designed for them either.

But the emphasis began to shift in 2010 with the breakout success of the Foursquare app. The current emphasis is to connect people by geography as well as affinity. Instagram plays in this space brilliantly, working to connect people by interests and by locations. Local businesses have an opportunity to enhance their interaction with their community in a new and exciting way using Instagram. Let's look at the ways local businesses can leverage the local nature of Instagram.

1. **Set up your location.** If you haven't done it yet, be sure to create your location via Facebook. The help article is horrendous, so I'll encourage you to simply google, "Facebook how do I create a new location." Seven steps later, you're all set. We are just in the very early days of utilizing geotags for local marketing. The initial effort is simply to have prospective customers share with their friends about their interactions with your business.

2. **Photo walks.** A photo walk is just what you might imagine—people joining together to walk and take pictures. You meet up, walk around, take pictures, and have a good time with other photographers. Most photo walks are done in an area that is tourist focused, say, downtown in a big city or in a getaway or vacation spot. If you're running a business in one of those spots, then you can coordinate photo walks that start and stop at your establishment. It's an easy way to meet new prospective customers.

3. **In-event sharing.** Any time you conduct an activity like a special event, fund-raiser, summer picnic, or even just a regular Sunday church service, you have the opportunity to include participants in the event by having them share images using a hashtag. Simply announce the hashtag in your promotional materials and let the crowd do the rest.

4. **Social rally.** Do you need to mobilize a special event like a rally, sporting event, or concert? A special hashtag will allow all the participants to tag their photos so they can be shared by all. Your job is simply to create the hashtag.

5. **Local contests.** Lots of photo contests can be done online in various formats. But there isn't any reason why a contest cannot be done locally, too. (More on contests in Step 11.)

6. **Coupons and special offers.** If you're a local business, give away a free item on a certain day and time. See how powerful your Instagram advertising can get. Learn to use Instagram for this type of direct marketing and integrate it into your business calendar. Launching a new product? Give away a secondary item for free at the same time to draw a large crowd.

Staying open later in the summer? Give away a special gift for people who visit in the last hour of your new schedule each day for the first week.

7. **Influencer review.** In Step 16 we'll dig into how to work with influencers. One of the most common ways for local marketers is to offer a freebie in exchange for a social mention.

Behind the Scenes with Mike Cooch

In San Diego, local marketer Mike Cooch (@michaelcooch on Instagram) is working with merchants to get them up and running on Instagram. You can learn more about his local agency at http://digitalmarketinglab.io. I asked him to share his insights on local marketing with us. Here is the Q&A:

Q: Tell us a little bit about your business—what do you do?

A: I publish an online guide to the best to eat, drink, see, and do in San Diego. I also offer sales and marketing training programs online and run a content marketing agency.

Q: How do you see local businesses uniquely leveraging Instagram successfully? Any example stories you can share?

A: Instagram is *the* hot social app in local, no question! In San Diego, and I think in most cities at this point, all of the influence regarding the hottest restaurants, bars, parties, etc. comes from local influencers on Instagram. One business here in San Diego that has particularly impressed me with their use of Instagram is a local kayak tour shop, on Instagram @everydaycalifornia (see Figure 5.3). They've used Instagram to promote the Southern California lifestyle, which allowed them to translate their brand into a clothing line that has taken off.

Q: Why do you think Instagram is working so well for local businesses right now compared to other options?

Figure 5.3 Everyday California

A: Because it's naturally very local in nature, and because there isn't much noise. I say it's "local in nature" because aside from the major brands and influencers, 99 percent of people are using it to capture the things they see and do every day, which means it's local! And it just doesn't have all of the noise of Facebook, which makes it very easy to connect with people on the platform. I think it's the platform where people are by far most receptive to a cold contact.

Q: You seem to particularly like IG Stories compared to posting photos for businesses; can you tell us why?

A: Yeah I do, for several reasons.

1. They are temporary, so if you are doing anything promotional it doesn't sit on your feed and broadcast that you have a promotional account.

2. You can tell much more of a story.

3. You can link from the story to other websites (after you have 10,000 followers), making it a good traffic source.

4. It's much more informal in nature, again because it's not a part of the feed. That gives me the opportunity to just have a little more fun with it, which is more natural to me than trying to create the perfect picture.

Q: Are there three or four tips you'd offer for local businesses trying to leverage the power of Instagram?

1. Commit to it! Don't dabble . . . get in there and get busy and stick with it.

2. Be authentic—don't post just to try to be cool on Instagram. Have your own voice and perspective.

3. Keep in mind that it's a community. Reach out to people, make connections, like their content, comment on their content, share their content. Do all of the things on IG that you would do offline to build a relationship, and treat your IG relationships like you would treat good offline relationships. Don't just ask for stuff or make offers . . . have conversations and add value without expectation of immediate return.

4. Be interesting. This is a creative stretch for a lot of businesses that don't really have a "marketer" at the helm, but it's how you really stand out on IG. Invest time brainstorming interesting visual stories you can tell that may (but not necessarily) incorporate your products and services.

Q: Are there any third-party tools or other products you use to support your Instagram efforts?

A: I like Later. It's a nice posting/scheduling app that I can use from desktop or phone. They are 100 percent focused on IG, so they have it pretty dialed in.

Q: If people want your help with local Instagram marketing, how can they connect?

A: I'm on Instagram at @michaelcooch—follow me and send me a DM!

Marketing a Service on Instagram

Service providers have a unique story to tell and a distinct way they market themselves. The truth is, service providers must sell their services, but they must also sell themselves. The customer is buying a long-term relationship, and the quality of the long-term relationship directly impacts the overall impression of the service being provided. There are lots of ways to do it. Let's go behind the scenes with a creative service provider to get her insider tips.

Behind the Scenes with Sydney Paulsen

As I was working on this chapter I said to myself, who do I know that is a service provider that is crushing it on Instagram? Then I looked up and saw Sydney, our freelance photographer. She visits our office every Tuesday to do our product photography—she crushes it for us! You can see her work @5hensandacockatiel. She's also worked with major brands such as Mattel and AMCTV. She got those gigs through Instagram. I asked her to share her story with us—here's the Q&A:

Q: Tell us a little bit about your business?

A: I'm a photographer, specializing in doll and product photography, based in Seattle, Washington (see Figure 5.4). Most of my clientele are companies that make doll clothing and furniture; they pay me to photograph their products.

Q: That's pretty unique. How did you get started, and how did Instagram play a part?

Figure 5.4 Sydney Rose

A: In 2013, I began posting daily photos of my American Girl dolls, which had always been a hobby of mine. Through years of consistent uploading and always striving to improve the quality of my photos, I started to attract a large following in the doll community. In 2015, small companies began reaching out and commissioning me (small scale) to photograph their products and post the photos on my Instagram to advertise their products to my followers. From there, I was able to make multiple connections (PixieFaire/ LibertyJane, Little Gloriana, A Girl for All Time, Olivia's Little World, The Queen's Treasures, and American Girl Brand, along with many others).

Q: What's been the benefit of using Instagram—any business relationships or partnerships that you can share about?

A: Instagram makes it incredibly simple to make connections with people and companies that I never dreamed were possible. Most brands have realized that Instagram is an incredible opportunity to connect with followers on a much more personal level. I've noticed that companies especially love it when you tag them in your picture—it's free advertising for them, and they can see people's honest reactions and reviews of their products. Because of this, followers have a lot more power than I think they realize.

A dream of mine has always been to work with American Girl (the doll company which inspired my Instagram account in the first place), and by reaching out to them in a direct message and becoming familiar with each other through our IG accounts, that dream came true in 2017 when they asked me if I'd be willing to help them promote their newest contemporary character, Z Yang.

I was also able to work with AMCTV in September of 2017, when their photo editor reached out to me and asked if I'd be willing to create and shoot a series of photos of *The Walking Dead* using Funko Pop! dolls to promote the show's upcoming season (see Figure 5.5). I received this job because of another Instagram connection I'd made through working with the girls and dolls clothing brand Little Gloriana, while on an insanely cool and unexpected business trip to New York. I can safely say that none of this would have ever happened had I never started my Instagram account.

Figure 5.5 Doll Photo Promo for *The Walking Dead*

Q: For photographers or other service providers who want to begin using Instagram, what advice would you share?

A: Post consistently and constantly reach out to different brands you admire, showing them what you can do *for them*. Whenever I've landed a job that I really wanted, the result usually came about by me reaching out to the company directly and providing them with a portfolio of my work customized to their needs. Once you've established a few client relationships that you particularly value, you can keep referring back to the work you do for them to promote your future endeavors with prospective new customers.

Q: Are there other social media or marketing tools you use—and how do they compare to Instagram?

A: I've tried posting my work and creating a following on Facebook, but it's certainly a different medium entirely! I haven't had nearly as much luck accruing the engagement and response as I have on Instagram. Insta makes it so, so easy to communicate with your followers and reach others (within and outside of the community).

Q: Is it hard to connect with prospective clients on Instagram?

A: If you're wanting to connect with anyone—not just me—don't simply try one avenue. Especially with influencers who have a larger following, it's difficult to keep up with all of the notifications. If I have learned anything from my work, it's to be persistent. Reach out over DM and email, if an address is listed, and wait a week. If the person you're trying to contact doesn't respond, it's always good to have a backup avenue of persistent contact methods up your sleeve!

Q: How can people connect with you?

A: The best way to get in contact with me is following my Instagram account and sending me a DM @5hensandacockatiel or @sydney.rose.studios.

Whether you're a nonprofit, local marketer, or service provider, your work matters, and by serving others you're making a huge difference in your community and beyond. In Part II we'll focus on creating a powerful content strategy, forming a daily action plan, and building a support team.

SNAPSHOT

1. Instagram can work really well for nonprofits, local marketers, and service providers.

2. You're selling a relationship and connection—and Instagram is a great tool for it.

3. Take Sydney's advice and be persistent.

4. Begin collecting or creating the images that will help you tell your unique story.

Part II

O = ORGANIZE YOUR MESSAGE

Good order is the foundation of all things.

EDMUND BURKE

Create Your Content Blueprint

Setting goals is the first step in turning the invisible into the visible.

TONY ROBBINS
@tonyrobbins on Instagram

The hardest question each Instagram user must answer is, *What is my content-sharing strategy, and how does it deliver value to my tribe members on a daily basis?* Answering that question is central to your success on the platform. In this chapter, we'll give you a logical blueprint to build your own unique content that you can take action on daily.

If you want a nicely formatted PDF version of the Content Blueprint that you can print and use, visit www.winning.online and snag the free Instagram Power Expansion Pack PDF. The blueprint will give you a single-page overview of the entire process. The PDF will also be particularly helpful if you are going to use a team for your Instagram efforts. We'll dive into how to do that in the next chapter. Just print it out, fill it in, and look like a well-organized leader!

Let's walk through the elements of a professional content strategy that your tribe will love. One word of encouragement: Don't feel like you have to master all of this from the start. Just begin implementing and learning—that's the goal.

The blueprint has three logical components that you want to work on. First, you need to choose your topical themes. Second, you need to formalize the visual style—the look and feel of your content. Finally, you need to decide which Instagram publishing option to use for each content piece you share.

Framework Step One: Clarify Your Themes

The best Instagram profiles publish content that has a feel, vibe, or emotional element to it. Generally, it is two or three thematic ideas that the Instagrammer repeats frequently. Let's call those ideas *content themes*. These smart marketers revisit their themes over and over again in creative ways. But the themes are consistent, they stay on-topic and focused, and the marketers' tribes clearly love them for it. So, step one in the framework is committing to several themes. I'd recommend you choose three, but how many you focus on is up to you.

Example Themes

Ideally, you'll have some unique themes that are custom tailored to you and your tribe. Your words—your ideas. But sometimes we get stuck. To make it easy, I've included a few examples from successful Instagrammers, and a list of 25 common themes.

Example #1: University of Washington. The University of Washington brand management team has a terrific set of public documents outlining how they uphold their brand across all social and media channels. (See Figure 6.1.)

I'd encourage you to study all of their public content on the subject at: http://www.washington.edu/brand/editorial-elements/monthly -themes/. Three of their themes include:

- Proven Impact
- Innovation Mindset
- Be Boundless

Figure 6.1 University of Washington

Example #2: Lewis Howes. *New York Times* bestselling author of *School of Greatness* Lewis Howes has a terrific Instagram content strategy on Instagram @lewishowes (Figure 6.2). He describes his themes as:

- Grow
- Share
- Encourage

Example #3: Gary Vaynerchuk. Ranked as Forbes #1 Business Influencer, Gary Vee recently wrote an article, "My Content Is a Mindset!," about his view of content and themes. In it he talks about why he publishes different types of content on different platforms. I'd encourage you to read it at https://www.garyvaynerchuk.com/mindset/. See Figure 6.3.

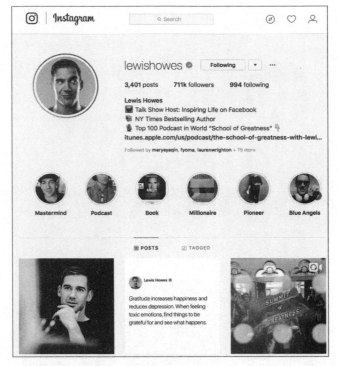

Figure 6.2 Lewis Howes

Here is an excerpt that expresses his view of themes well:

Everyday, I put out content around the 25–47 themes I con-tinually express. I'm always talking about gratitude, empathy, self-awareness, legacy, hustle, humility, and everything else. . . . The bottom line is real simple. I'm trying to be here every day for everybody and bring value to you guys so that all of you can feed off of my energy and optimism, and find strength in my communi-cation style in order to instill confidence in you, or give you courage.

There is a lot there, but notice the last few words. He tries to have energy and optimism in order to provide:

- Strength
- Confidence
- Courage

Figure 6.3 Gary Vaynerchuk

20 Themes to Consider

Here is a brief list of 20 example themes you might consider. These should align nicely with your core brand and really resonate with who you are and what you can deliver in service to your tribe. Strive to make them uniquely yours in some interesting way. I've included an additional 80 theme ideas in the Expansion Pack, so you'll have 100 to consider.

Business

- Inspirational quotes
- Innovation
- Overcoming the odds
- Teamwork
- Patience

Personal Health

- Health quotes / wisdom
- Recipes
- Fitness
- Attitude
- Friendship

Science and Nature

- Amazing animals
- Struggle to survive
- Sustainability
- Science / Technology
- Astronomy / Space

Spiritual

- Faith
- Love
- Wisdom
- Peace
- Hope

Remember, you want to share things your tribe will appreciate seeing, not things that simply make you feel good. Posting for their benefit, not your own, is the secret ingredient. You also want them to like it so much they share it and follow you so they get more.

One goal of creating a content strategy, and clarifying it early and often, is that it will allow you to stay consistent in your sharing behavior over time, which instills confidence in your followers. Conventional wisdom says that you should take a quality-over-quantity approach to your content sharing on Instagram. But you'll have to decide what that means for your situation and whether it is the right approach for your followers. Maybe they need all the encouragement they can get as quickly as possible, in whatever form you want to give it to them, regardless of whether it looks polished or unpolished!

Additionally, now that Instagram is heavily invested in video content, you'll have to decide on the mix between photos and videos. You'll want to consider:

- How frequently you should share content? My suggestion is at least one post a day.

- What types of content are you going to focus on? My suggestion is to share things that impress, inspire, motivate, educate, or otherwise benefit your ideal followers. If it gives them value—you're on the right track.

- What times of the day or night are you going to share content?

- Are there quality or editorial standards you are going to impose on your work?

- Who gets to post content, who approves it, and who implements the overall long-term plan?

There is a reason your prospective new Instagram followers will tap "follow." To point out the obvious—they saw something in your profile or content strategy that they liked, and they want to see more of it. Do you know what it is?

Framework Step Two: Clarify Your Visual Style

Your Instagram feed will ideally have a visual style that is consistent, engaging, and connected nicely to your overall brand strategy. You'll notice that in our Content Blueprint framework, the biggest pie wedge is tied to the content themes. That's because it's the biggest deal. Get it right and you can afford to be less focused on the visual style issues. Don't get me wrong, they are important, but less important than the content themes. What's included in visual style?

When most people think of branding, they think of the visible aspects. These include:

- **Name.** The name is one of the single most important aspects of the brand. A good name can help a business or product be memorable, interesting, and fun to say. A bad name can make it impossible to even pronounce the business or product, much less say anything nice about it.

- **Logo.** Your logo is the visible symbol of your company. There are three basic options: text, a symbol, or a combination of the two.

- **Tagline.** Taglines give you the opportunity to install a little statement or jingle into your prospect's mind—"Red Bull Gives You Wings," "Just Do It," "Like a Good Neighbor, State Farm Is There." A tagline can add real power to your message.

- **Color palette.** Your brand can benefit from a consistent and well-put-together color palette. The opportunity to have a color associated with your brand adds a visual element that helps distinguish you from your competition.

- **Typeface.** Your font choice says something about your brand. It can indicate that you are a fun and informal company or that you are a formal and conservative establishment. Do your best to establish harmony among your typeface, brand persona, and the other visible elements of your brand.

- **Graphics style.** Your customers and prospects can interpret a lot about you by your use of graphics. Are you a young, hip company or a savvy, intellectual firm? Your graphics might answer that question.

A Photography Skills Resource

Let me refer you to one online resource to further your education as it relates to photography—Karl Taylor, on Instagram @karltaylor photography, and on the web at www.karltayloreducation.com. His YouTube training videos are fantastic.

Let's review a few of the basic concepts of photography briefly:

- **Composition.** The composition or layout of the image can radically change how people perceive it. The same scene can result in an amazing picture or a boring one, depending on how the photographer arranges the visual elements.

- **Lighting.** Your lighting will be different for product photography versus other types of photography. Mastering lighting is one of the keys to effective photography. Most commonly, natural light produces a nicer result than indoor lighting.

- **Subject matter.** Having an interesting subject is the most important part of any photo. The biggest challenge most photographers face is trying to identify interesting subject matter.

- **Simplicity.** Many times, photographs are made more interesting by what is left out, rather than what is included. Cropping out irrelevant elements and allowing the viewer to focus on just one aspect of the scene will improve most images.

- **Focal point.** Having a single focal point is part of striving for simplicity. The question for every image is, *What will people be drawn toward within the image, and how can I prominently position that part?*

- **Perspective.** You have the opportunity to tell a story with your images. Your perspective is unique, and the way you take the photo reflects that uniqueness. For example, when you're standing in an orchard, you can focus on the strict order of the tree planting, the leaves or bark on the tree, or a bird on a branch. Each is a different perspective on the same orchard.

- **Point of view.** The angle at which you take a picture can affect the final result dramatically. Many times, simply raising the camera up higher or kneeling down can change the point of view enough to move an image from boring to interesting.

- **Filters.** Instagram was designed to allow iPhone photographers to edit and share their images. The filters included in the app allow you to substantially alter your photos. How you do that can either make them look brilliant and inviting or cause them to look "off" and "wrong." Over time, you'll come to use different filters for different situations.

- **Black and white versus color.** One of the simplest ways to increase the interest in a photo is by making it black and white instead of color. Instagram has several filters that allow you to do different versions of black and white.

- **Unedited or filtered.** There is a "purist" tribe of users within Instagram that has a real disdain for filters. They would much rather see images that are high quality and unedited than lower quality and edited heavily. You'll have to choose which perspective you want to take on.

- **Sharpness.** Most mobile phones allow you to focus on several areas on the screen before you take the picture, and by doing so you can alter the sharpness of the focal point or make things intentionally less sharp.

- **Depth of field.** A common technique in portrait and product photography is the concept of a shallow depth of field—having the focal point in your image be closer to the camera and in focus and having the background be intentionally unfocused. While older smartphone cameras cannot create this effect out of the box, as you might guess, there's an app for that! Try SynthCam for the iPhone.

- **Color saturation.** A common issue with images is that they are not as vibrant as they could be. The Photoshop Express app helps you resolve this issue and many other common issues mentioned in this section.

Videography Skill Resource

Videography is a trade skill that could take countless books and courses to cover. To get up to speed quickly and affordably, let me recommend another resource, Video School Online, www.videoschoolonline.com. Founder Phil Ebner has taught over 750,000 students worldwide and is ranked as one of the most popular instructors on Udemy. With over 75 courses, and 300 tutorials, you'll find plenty to help expand your videography skills on the site.

Framework Step Three: Select Your Publishing Method

The next logical step in the Content Blueprint framework is to master the appropriate publishing options and clarify which one you want to use for any given content piece. I'll outline the big idea in this chapter, then in the next chapter I'll provide a Content Blueprint Daily Actions checklist. Truth is, the whole thrust of this book is built around the idea of turning your Instagram posts into micro marketing activities. Each post is a brick in the wall of a larger campaign. Each campaign has a goal. Each goal ties to a business objective. Let's look at your options, then talk about how to integrate them into your blueprint in a systematic way.

Instagram Publishing Methods

The list of Instagram publishing methods is growing all the time. Your job is to identify a plausible marketing activity using each one—and your method needs to be done in harmony with your visual style and in support of one of your topical themes. Instagram publishing methods currently include the following, but don't be surprised if more are made available after this book is in print:

- Feed a single photo (the oldest part of the matrix)

- Feed multiple photos in one post

- Feed video (up to 60 seconds)

- Instagram story photo(s) (exists for only 24 hours)

- Instagram story boomerang video (1 second) (exists for only 24 hours)

- Instagram story video (up to 15 seconds) (exists for only 24 hours)

- Instagram Story Highlight (preserves story content and strings it together)

- IGTV (up to 10 minutes for most accounts, up to an hour for larger accounts)

Content Blueprint Inception

Sorry to go all *Inception* on you, but you need to take the whole blueprint down a level and create a content strategy for each of the primary Instagram publishing options. If you do only photos now, take it down a level and build a plan for feed videos. If you do photos and videos, take it down another level and build a plan for Stories. Then another level for Story Highlights. Keep going deeper until you have a content strategy for each publishing option on Instagram. The better you utilize all the publishing options, the more powerful your Instagram marketing becomes. The better your content is aligned with your themes and resonates with your audience, the stronger your marketing becomes.

Just Ask, "What Would Leonardo Do?"

A fantastic example of this principle is actor, and star of the movie *Inception*, Leonardo DiCaprio (on Instagram @leonardodicaprio—see Figure 6.4). Although he doesn't use all the Instagram publishing options, he aligns his content with his topic themes perfectly. In his bio he describes himself as an Actor and Environmentalist. What you'll find on his account is an occasional actor-related post, and a large number of environmentalist videos and photos. The environmental videos, in particular, are powerful. So from the bio to the daily posts he is aligning his topics and using both photos and videos brilliantly to support the ideas. He already has over 25 million followers—imagine if he started doing Instagram Live videos, Stories, or created Story Highlights.

If you ignore this step in the publishing process and don't consider all the options, it's like your car engine not firing on all cylinders. For example, Instagrammers that have avoided using Instagram Stories over the last few years have missed out on a huge aspect of Instagram user content consumption and a terrific method for exposure and account growth. I'll admit, I'm one of those people. I just didn't realize I was making that mistake over the last few years as I shied away from doing Story content. I didn't have a strategy for it—so I didn't so it. Learn from my mistake.

Figure 6.4 Leonardo DiCaprio

Creative Content Strategies

There are tried-and-true content styles that you should look into. Let's review a few of them. We'll break the list into two—photo styles and then video styles.

Photo Styles

1. **Create a grid layout.** For a creative photo option that allows you to design the overall look of your Instagram feed, check out the Preview app at https://thepreviewapp.com. This is particularly interesting for fashion or beauty Instagrammers.

2. **Motivational or inspirational quotes.** These are a mainstay on Instagram business accounts for three simple reasons—they give something of value to the reader, they are easy to make, and they are nearly limitless in supply. When you are wondering which

would be better to post—a selfie or an inspirational quote—well, you know the answer. Consider using the following free tools to make the magic happen. Quotes from www.brainyquotes.com, free high-resolution professional images from burst.shopify.com, and nice font and layout options from www.canva.com. This trifecta will have you creating inspirational quotes like a machine!

3. **Shoppable Posts.** If you're a retailer of physical products, then this is a must. These are done as photos in the feed. More on this in Step 12.

4. **User generated content.** If you have fans or followers that share something that has merit for broader distribution, ask them if you can use it.

5. **Product photography.** Don't forget to show images of your products, but keep it interesting. The flat lay style, where images are shot from directly overhead in a creative way, is most popular. But you can also show "lifestyle" photos where your products are in use.

6. **Ad-like images.** Need to widely distribute a coupon code? Create something that looks like an ad. We'll dive into this method more deeply in Step 12.

7. **Giveaways and contests.** Contests are a great way to move people to action. We'll share more on this in Step 11.

8. **"We're hiring" posts.** Have an open spot on your team? Sharing about it on Instagram leverages your fans and followers and also let's them know you're growing!

9. **Throwback images.** The Instagram tradition is to share a throwback image every Thursday using the hashtag #tbt. Be creative and find ways to educate your customers about your company!

10. **Using Creative Commons content.** In an upcoming chapter, we'll discuss the proper use of user generated content, or UGC—that is, images that your fans or followers created. We'll also talk about the ethical way to repost other people's content when that makes sense to do. But a third option is to use what is known as Creative Commons licensed content. This is possible because there is a category of Creative Commons for commercial use of the content.

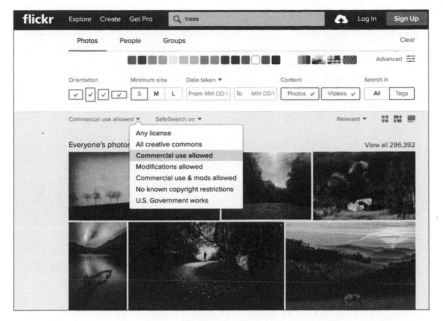

Figure 6.5 Flickr

Frequently, the photographers involved will ask for attribution, which means you give appropriate credit to the photographer when you post it. Fair enough! These images are great for using under quotes, or simply as stand-alone images if they align with your content themes. You can find high-quality Creative Commons content on numerous sites. I like Flickr, www.flickr.com (see Figure 6.5).

Video Styles to Experiment With

Both Stories and IGTV are game changers for Instagram marketing. Now you can craft very intentional video content for the platform and have it shared effectively. Your video length falls into four buckets:

- Shortest—Boomerang (1 second), then Instagram Stories (15 seconds)

- Medium—Instagram feed (60 seconds)

- Longer—IGTV (10 minutes, and longer for larger accounts)

- Live video—Up to one hour

1. **The candid video.** Do a Live video—it can be up to an hour. Share passionately about one of your content themes, and publish. Rinse and repeat.

2. **Boomerang.** Can you do split-second marketing? Yes! To see how I use clips in an on-topic way, visit my profile @mrjasonmiles.

3. **The About Us video.** Why make people read your About Us page on your website when you can make a video out of it? This can be low budget if it's thoughtful and tasteful. Or you can hire a local videographer to make it nice. You can also save this in your Story Highlights so new visitors can find it quickly.

4. **The FAQ video.** Answer your customers' most common questions live on camera. Take the time to explain things about your product, service, or organization.

5. **The animated explainer video.** These are sticky because they are designed to be brief, informative, and visually interesting. For a low-priced option try www.fiverr.com, or for a more upscale version, try www.videoexplainers.com. See how we use one @sewpowerful in the "Join Us" Story Highlight.

6. **How-to videos.** Do you have a product that needs to be explained or demonstrated? Make sure you've got your how-to videos on Instagram. Yes, these used to typically reside on YouTube, but with the launch of IGTV, Instagram is clearly making a play for this type of content.

7. **Customer testimonial videos.** If you can encourage your customers to make you a testimonial video, it can be worth its weight in gold. String four or five together and you've got massive social proof.

8. **Keynotes or formal events.** Do you have video from keynotes addresses that you've delivered? Maybe conference talks or special events? Post them!

9. **Tip of the Week video.** Consider making a Tip of the Week video. We do ours via Facebook Live and then repurpose the content.

Tools to Stich Together Your Story Highlights

One nice workaround people are using effectively is to take longer videos, use an app called Cutstory (there are others such as Continual App or Storeo) to effectively cut your video into 15-second clips, then upload them sequentially as Story content, then save them as Story Highlights. What you end up with is a longer Story Highlight video that plays fairly nicely, with a minor pause every 15 seconds. Not ideal, but it works.

Now that we've covered the basics, it's time to learn from the master. Wondering how you can take one piece of longer video content and turn it into an explosion of tribe-centric posts? Let's take this to a much deeper level with Gary Vaynerchuck.

The GaryVee Content Machine Method

The sage of social and founder of Vayner Media, Gary Vaynerchuk, has a how-to guide for creating content that he generously shares on his Instagram profile, @garyvee. I'd encourage you to watch the entire presentation. We'd all be wise to listen and learn from him. With over 3.9 million Instagram followers, he is the authority on the subject. You can also view the full 86-slide deck at https://www.slideshare.net /vaynerchuk/the-garyvee-content-model-107343659.

His model, in summary, includes the following elements:

1. **Pillar content.** One piece of "pillar content" shared each day. This might be a keynote address, a documentary his team makes about his day, a video recording of his Q&A show, or a podcast he's done, etc.

2. **Micro content.** His team repurposes the content into short-form pieces, (memes, GIFs, quotes, stories, etc.). They take the highlights or best moments and will create up to 30 smaller content pieces a day. They focus on moments that they think will resonate well with his audience.

3. **Broad distribution.** The short-form pieces are distributed across a wide range of social media platforms, each tailor-made for their ideal platform format. Images with quotes for Instagram, 15-second clips for Instagram Stories, longer

content for IGTV, and a nice collection of other micro pieces for sites like Facebook, LinkedIn, Twitter, Quora, YouTube, Snapchat, etc. They include images, video, and articles. They are designed to lead people to the pillar content and generate viewership, readership, and listenership.

4. **Listen to your audience.** His team watches for audience feedback, collects insights, and then adapts the micro content further based on audience engagement.

5. **Publish second round of micro content.** After creating revised micro content, they modify it further and distribute the newly revised pieces broadly on all the social platforms mentioned in step 3.

In his presentation, Gary demonstrates how one long-form content piece, a keynote address, resulted in 35 million views across 20 different platforms. Even if you can't reproduce his method in its entirety given your time and team constraints, it's a great explanation of how a top content producer creates a huge impact, and serves as a great model.

In the next chapter, we'll look at how you can begin to actively engage with your ideal tribe members. But remember, it all starts with a powerful profile and a targeted content strategy. If you don't have these basic marketing strategies well designed, nothing else matters.

SNAPSHOT

1. Use the Powerful Profile Checklist to create a professional profile that serves as your Instagram home page.

2. Develop your content strategy to consistently produce content your tribe will love.

3. Consider using the GaryVee Content Machine Method.

Use the Daily Actions Checklist to Gather Your Tribe

If you don't find the time, if you don't do the work, you don't get the results.

ARNOLD SCHWARZENEGGER
@schwarzenegger on Instagram

Now that you've got a powerful profile and a clear content strategy, it's time to find your tribe and get connected with them in a meaningful way. This chapter will explain the best practices for growing your tribe, then in the next chapter we'll discuss strategies for building your Instagram support team. It's time to go on the offense, get out and connect directly with people, and build your tribe.

Of course, we all want to grow our tribe to a large number. But the total number of followers isn't everything. Engaged followers are better than unengaged followers. So the ideal mix is a large number of followers who are also highly engaged. That's the goal.

Followers = Social Proof

Like it or not, on Instagram and other social sites, the number of followers you have is a status symbol and visual display of social proof of popularity. It's oftentimes the first thing people look at. Are you a big deal? Look to the number of followers. Should they partner with you? Look to the number of followers. Do you command respect and admiration? Look to the number of followers. Like it or not, this is the game, and we have to figure out how to win.

The Follow-Like-Comment-Respond (FLCR) Method

The tried-and-true method of building your profile's followership is commonly referred to as the Follow-Like-Comment-Respond or FLCR method. The idea is simple. Follow people, like their content, and make comments. If you do, the chances of them following you go up exponentially, especially when you do these three activities in a focused way, following someone's account, liking some of their content, and leaving a comment. The reason is simple—you get on their radar, so they look at your account and take the time to decide if following you is a good idea. Of course, you can do the following, liking, and commenting as stand-alone activities separate from each other. Let's look at each of these ideas in further detail.

Following People and Business Profiles

Before we mention the groups to consider following, let me discuss how best to actually do this work. The first step you can take is to begin following others in small batches of 40 to 50. By following them in batches and waiting a few days, you'll see who follows you back. If people follow you back, then you should consider them interested in you, your products, or your company. Or at least consider them favorably inclined toward the images you've shared in your feed and the description you've created for your profile. This is generally referred to on Twitter as a follow-to-be-followed strategy, and it works very well on Instagram.

After you determine whether these people are going to follow you or not, you can unfollow the people who didn't follow you; and in that way, you can keep the overall number of people you're following fairly similar to the number of people following you. Then you simply "rinse and repeat." It should be noted: not everyone appreciates this tactic.

Of course, if you join Instagram and follow 5,000 people but only have 5 followers, you will look like a spammer. So you want to gradually control the number of people you follow and keep it in relative proportion to the number of people following you. Ideally, you'll have more followers than people that you follow.

Seven Groups to Consider Following

But who should you be following? The list is long and unique to each of us, but I'll mention some top ideas. The main lesson here is—be strategic. Don't just follow random people—use this as a sorting function to get closer to your ideal tribe members. Here are a few groups to consider:

1. **Your existing followers on other platforms,** Facebook being the easiest. Asking your existing fans and followers to join you on Instagram is the first step in building your profile. Inviting your friends and followers from other platforms to follow you on Instagram gets you an initial set of followers so you don't look like a spammer as you begin to follow other people.

2. **People following the hashtags associated with your industry.** Follow people using the hashtags associated with your industry, niche, or product. Now, they may be your competitors, so you'll have to sort through that. But if you can follow people who are hobbyists or industry enthusiasts using this technique, do it. You never know how influential these people are—maybe they run a trade group, Facebook group, local meet-up, or similar group. Their connection to you could unlock lots of potential followers.

3. **People following your competition.** This may or may not work well depending on how loyal they are to the other brand—so watch for backlash.

4. **People following authors who write about your industry or niche.** If there are gurus, teachers, or leaders in your space, chances are they've got who you want.

5. **People following websites,** consumer-focused magazines, or publications in your niche.

6. **Follow your customers.** This can be tricky, but if it makes sense and doesn't seem socially odd in your context, follow your customers.

7. **Follow the friends of your followers.** You'll have to decide if following your friends' friends is a good idea for your business, niche, or industry. If you're a local restaurant, the answer is probably yes since many people's friends are located in the same city. If you sell a product where the friends of your followers are not necessarily going to be prospects, then skip this group.

Let's consider the math. As an example of how your initial following work can lead to a second generation of people to follow, let's say 100 of your existing customers join Instagram, and they begin following you. Let's say that each of them has 25 followers, and they also follow a different group of 25 people. When you add it all up, that is 5,000 people who you know are associated with your current customers. If you follow them over time, and even a fraction of them follow you back, you're making progress.

Liking Images

The second social action in the FLCR method is to like images or videos that are shared by the people you've followed. Liking content is the fastest and easiest way to get noticed by prospective customers. Simply like a few of their photos, and they'll notice you. It's like introducing yourself in a friendly way. If you want to grow your followership very quickly, begin liking tons of content. Don't underestimate the power of simply liking people's content. You will add hundreds, if not thousands, of followers if you faithfully like pictures every day.

The nice part about liking people's images is that it will get you noticed, but it does not have the negative consequences associated with following a lot of people. In other words, people won't accuse you of being a spammer if you simply like 200 pictures a day. There is no social downside.

> **POWER TIP**
>
> Don't just post a picture and wait for people to start follow-ing you. Make it your goal to follow good prospects, like lots of pictures every day, and leave positive comments. Be proac-tive socially, and you'll see your profile grow quickly.

Why is liking so important? People are focused on themselves, and as the old saying goes, "People don't care how much you know until they know how much you care." Liking shows them that you care. It also shows them that you approve of their content and their profile. Liking makes people feel good about their Instagram work. You've given them something, and the law of reciprocity is likely to kick in. They will consider following you and liking your work—espe-cially if your profile is a powerful magnet and your content strategy is tailor-made to give them value.

An easy way to quickly like an image is to simply double tap on it. This functionality works nicely in the Instagram app. Unfortunately, there is no equivalent on the website version. On the website, you must click on the image and then click the Like button.

Leaving Comments

The next action in the FLCR method is to leave a comment. Leave a sincere compliment, ask a question about the picture, or make a statement related to the picture. This behavior is not unwelcomed on Instagram, and if you're being sincere, it is a fantastic way to get your name in front of a lot of people. Not only will the person who owns the image notice you, but the person's friends who like the image will also see your comment and take notice.

As with the follow-to-be-followed strategy, you want to be very intentional about the images you are leaving comments on. Be focused, be intentional, and be sincere.

Responding to People

Of course, you'll also want to respond to comments that people leave on your images. To respond quickly, simply hit Comment and then tap the person's comment (see Figure 7.1) and type a reply. You'll notice a gray slider that allows you to either type a reply or hit the Delete key. In this way you can leave a quick reply or quickly deal with spam comments.

Figure 7.1 Respond to Comments

In the early days Instagram didn't seem very conversational, but as it's grown, it has become a place for comments and responses. These occur on your posts, and the polite and savvy thing to do is respond to your comments. Create a dialogue. Engage with your tribe and build connections. You can also "like" every comment by tapping the heart sign next to it. That adds another layer of engagement—and lets people know you've seen their comments.

Daily Actions Checklist

The following checklist is provided to give you a daily practice to strive toward as it relates to both creating content and following, liking, commenting, and responding. It's not likely that you'll achieve each step every day, but you could. Of course, if you have an assistant, this can be his or her Instagram daily project plan. If you'd like a nicely formatted printable version of this checklist, be sure to visit www.winning.online and get the Expansion Pack. Make it your practice to do the following activities on Instagram each day:

- ☐ Post at least one picture.
- ☐ Post one boomerang, and turn these posts into a thematic Story Highlight over time.
- ☐ Do an Instagram Live, Story video, or IGTV video.
- ☐ Follow 40 to 50 people.
- ☐ Like 100 pictures.
- ☐ Leave comments on posts that use a top hashtag you are following.
- ☐ Unfollow 25 people who are not following you.
- ☐ Respond to any comments you receive and like them too.

A Fast and Affordable Way to Grow Your Instagram Followers with Influencers

In Step 16 we'll do a deep dive into influencer marketing strategies, but let me share one smart account growth-related tip from John Koch (on Instagram @theholydose), a marketer on the Tomoson Influencer platform, www.tomoson.com (see Figure 7.2).

John's strategy is genius, low cost, repeatable in any niche or industry, and effective. If you'd like to see the original post, titled "Sponsored Posts That Double Your Traffic and ROI," read more at https://blog.tomoson.com/instagram-marketing/sponsored-posts -that-double-your-traffic-and-roi/.

What follows is a summary of John's method:

1. Find a top influencer in your niche by looking at the relevant hashtags and the top posts. If you're not sure how to do that, don't worry—in Step 16 we'll discuss ways for researching influencers.

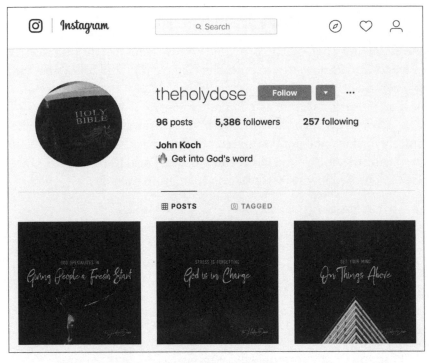

Figure 7.2 John Koch

2. When you have the influencer in mind, find the most liked post in the person's Instagram account.

3. Redo the post in a similar way in your own creative style. This is simplest if it's a quote, but be creative and think about why that person's audience liked that post.

4. Figure out a simple caption with a call to action that benefits you. In John's case, since his user name is @theholydose and he posts Bible verses every day, the call to action he came up with was "Follow @theholydose to get in God's word."

5. Armed with both a picture that you know will be effective and a call to action to follow your account, it's time to reach out to the influencer and see if he or she will post for you. When a blog reader asked John what he says in his DMs to influencers, he replied with the following example: "Hi Name! I'm John. Could I pay you for a shout-out to my Bible Images feed? If so,

how can I send you payment, image, and caption? I love how God is using your page to spread the message!"

6. Finalize the influencer posting details. Again, in Step 16, we'll discuss exactly how to find, vet, and professionally work with an influencer.

Of course, you'll have to adapt John's method to your own niche, but you get the idea. In summary, ask influencers to give you a shout-out and make it easy with content and copywriting that you know will resonate with their audience.

Tools for Management

As with the content creation and posting activities we discussed in the prior chapter, when it comes to the FLCR method efforts, busy entrepreneurs and business owners are quick to ask, how do I automate these tasks or delegate them? We are all busy. I get it. Delegating tasks to others makes a lot of sense—and there are also automation tools on the market that you can use. Let's explore a few of these options so you can decide how best to make the magic happen. In Step 18 we'll do a much broader review of the third-party tools available to help you manage your Instagram work.

Each of us will have a different view on how to get the work done, which is our duty as managers of our marketing effort. As long as we don't violate the Instagram terms of service, we can do things a lot of different ways. In my view, the highest ideal to strive for is to ensure the work is done daily. Just get it done. If that is happening, again within the bounds of Instagram's guidelines, then the "how" it gets done is less important.

If you're a solopreneur without the desire to add additional help, or maybe just passionate about managing the duties yourself, you get to do them all and decide if using tools to streamline the process is to your liking. Obviously, Michael Kors is not going to personally manage the Michael Kors Instagram profile (@michaelkors), which, incidentally, has 12.2 million followers and does a very nice job on Instagram. If you, similarly, have an individual or team helping you do your Instagram work, then you can give them the Daily Goals

Checklist and other details outlined in this chapter—and have them do the heavy lifting.

Let me also encourage you to look directly to Instagram for clarity on this topic. To find the full list of Instagram-approved third partners, visit https://business.instagram.com/partnerships/. I'd encourage you to follow Instagram's business blog at the same address so you know when it has made changes related to this topic. Let's look at just a few of the most popular partners so you get a feel for what they can do for you as it relates to publishing your content.

Hootsuite. The historical leader in the space, Hootsuite allows you to collaborate on content, then schedule it, publish it, analyze how it did, and more. Learn about it at https://hootsuite.com/instagram.

AgoraPulse. Focused on affordability and functionality, with AgoraPulse you can achieve the same functions as with Hootsuite, but you can also do much more. Learn more, and be sure to check out the "Compare" section in its footer at https://www.agorapulse.com.

Planoly. This is a visual planner for Instagram—and so much more! Trusted by over a million brands, business, and influencers, Planoly has a solid set of tools to consider—and a entry-level account is free! Learn more at: https://www.planoly.com.

SNAPSHOT

1. Instagram is not conversationally intensive, but it still requires social actions.

2. Learn methods for identifying and following good prospects.

3. Create activity goals for yourself so you can be proactive about connecting socially.

4. Never fall into the habit of just posting pictures without engaging socially.

Building Your Instagram Support Team

You can do what I cannot do.
I can do what you cannot do.
Together we can do great things.

MOTHER TERESA

We've already talked about creating a powerful profile, having a clear content strategy, and using the FLCR method to grow. But are there additional catalysts for growth that you can use? Short answer—yes! In this chapter, we'll discuss a set of strategies designed to put your Instagram profile growth on the fast track by building your Instagram support team. You can obviously hire talented helpers on the content creation side or on the account management (FLCR method) side. The choice is yours, and the options are almost endless. Let's review a few of them.

A Personal Note from GaryVee About Automation

Before we explore options for building your Instagram team, let me share a personal message I got from Gary Vaynerchuk a few years back. Hopefully this little story underscores the power of doing the work yourself in a genuine way. This isn't to say you shouldn't build a team, but it is an encouragement to do it wisely and be authentic as you go. Here's what happened.

I'll never forget following Gary on Twitter. I was on a trip to Sacramento in September 2013. Full disclosure, I wasn't a huge fan of either Twitter or GaryVee at the time. But my coworker at the time Alejandro Reyes, (@alejandroreyes on both Instagram and Twitter) said I had to follow Gary. I had to. (Sidenote: Alejandro has gone on to become a thriving influencer, which we'll discuss in Step 17.) So I said, "Okay, okay, yes, I'll follow GaryVee. He's already got hundreds of thousands of followers, but I'll join in." What happened next can only be described as a lesson on the power of doing the work yourself—and doing it with genuine care. Gary replied and said, "thnx for the follow man!" A cynic at heart, and assuming he had some automation tool that did that for him, I replied, "Wait, is this really you or some auto responder program? Impressed!" In reply, he did what only he would do—the stuff of legend. I received a reply from him, which contained a link (Figure 8.1).

I clicked on the link to discover he had recorded a video of himself from the backseat of a car in New York. On the video he simply said, "Jason, it's me. It's always really me."

Mind blown, and disrespect for GaryVee completely obliterated, I started laughing and said, "Alejandro, you'll never believe this" and showed him the video. Alejandro responded, "I told you bro—I told you—Gary is legit." He certainly is. Doing the work yourself is legit. Caring is legit. Real connections with real people are legit. With that said, let's look at your options for growing a team. Obviously, you can delegate some aspects of your effort but still stay engaged. The balance is entirely up to you.

Staffing Options

Here are some staffing options to consider:

1. **Online assistant.** Get an online assistant to help create your content and/or manage your account. On the content side, this works best for quotes, infographics, and related

Figure 8.1 GaryVee's Reply

content that doesn't require your constant involvement or personal photo taking. If you have to coordinate file sharing for both images and video, it becomes a bit more challenging, but even that isn't very difficult. Try www.freelancer.com or www.fiverr.com.

2. **Student or intern.** Hire a student or get an intern. This can work well because these people probably know a million times more about Instagram than you do—and if they are trying to build their résumé, then it is a win/win. Be sure to structure the deal fairly for both of you—but be sure to pay only for useable content, not work time. Depending on the situation, this might take a bit of work to set up at first, but after the intern understands and can help manage your content strategy, you should be all set.

3. **Local freelancer.** Hire a local photographer or videographer to help with content. This is a nice option because the freelancer can coordinate photo or video shoots around your schedule. As with the student or intern option, you'll need to optimize to pay for work produced, not for time. The other

entanglement you'll have to sort out is the ownership of the content. In general, you want to own the images or videos without restrictions on the use.

4. **Employee.** Assign it to an existing team member. This can work well if you have spare capacity on your team and someone who is passionate about Instagram. The challenge will be ensuring employees don't waste their time on Instagram all day—so get laser-beam-focused on daily duties and deliverables, and cap the time allowed to accomplish those tasks.

5. **Instagram influencers.** Instagram influencers will make content as part of their efforts—frequently you get to use it too. We'll share more about this option in Step 16.

Collaboration and Automation Tools

As mentioned, you can find the full list of approved third-party partners at: https://business.instagram.com/partnerships/. Obviously, your intern is not on Instagram's list of approved partners, nor is your part-time social media manager. So we'll have to apply some of our own logic when it comes to team building, delegation, and automation. Before we look at the options, let me mention a few principles I think each of us would be wise to ponder—first three for bosses, then three for employees (see box).

PRINCIPLES FOR BUSINESS OWNERS

1. **Organize the work carefully before delegating or automating.** Per Bill Gates (in Instagram @thisisbillgates, Figure 8.2), "The first rule of any technology used in a business is that automation applied to an efficient operation will magnify the efficiency. The second is that automation applied to an inefficient operation will magnify the inefficiency." So make sure your process for creating content and running your FLCR method is well organized and very clear.

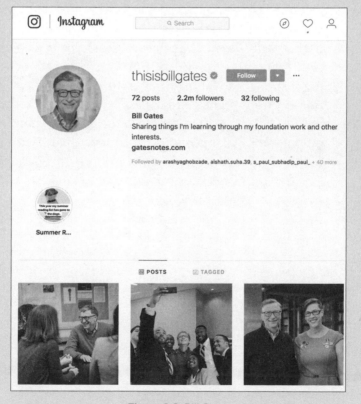

Figure 8.2 Bill Gates

2. **Delegating is not abdicating.** Understand the platform, process, and success principles involved well enough to effectively delegate. Then get the most competent and trustworthy person you can and let him or her execute your vision. If you're clueless, then at a minimum, have the person propose a plan to you, evaluate the merits, and then decide together. Ultimately, as the business owner, you're responsible for your helper's action on the platform.

3. **Using delegation or automation increases your risks.** You are responsible for your Instagram work. Including helpers, either people or software, increases the odds that something will go wrong. Chances are nothing will. But if you're the boss, then you're paid to worry about future negative outcomes. From offending customers, to PR nightmares, to wasting tons of money on ads (more on that soon), to getting kicked off the platform—the risks go up the more you hand off the work. So, as previously mentioned, work with competent people, employ ethical service providers, and take the time to ensure your actions are within the platform guidelines.

PRINCIPLES FOR EMPLOYEES DOING SOCIAL MEDIA DUTIES

1. **Educate your boss.** As a small-business owner employing social media workers, I can promise you—your help in educating the boss is truly needed. You've got a huge opportunity to explain how the Instagram world works. Take it. If your boss doesn't seem to care, find a way to speak his or her language. Try to focus on things your boss might care about most such as customer loyalty, customer testimonials, income, sales, leads, increased return on investment, and related top-of-mind topics. Bosses like hearing good news, so share it when you can.

2. **Don't let your boss order you to violate Instagram guidelines.** If your boss, through ignorance or willful bad behavior, tells you to violate Instagram guidelines, give a warning clearly and calmly, and make sure he or she understands the issue. Show the exact Instagram guidelines to make clear that it's not just your personal opinion. If your boss insists on the violation anyway, then you should resist, dust off your résumé, and start looking for a new gig. Connect with me on LinkedIn and I'll do my best to help you make a connection if I can.

3. **Ask your boss for tools.** Because automation and delegation methods increase business risk, which your boss is responsible for, it's really unwise to use these types of tools without getting approval. But if you can get your boss to approve helpful tools, do. Explain that you can be more efficient, manage more, and grow things faster with automation and delegation tools. Make the case as wisely as you can. If he or she says no, then live with that decision and do things in a less than optimal way.

Going Beyond the Instagram Approved List of Providers

There are a number of services you might want to look into that, although not on the third-party approved list, don't seem to violate the Instagram guidelines and do seem to offer a legitimate service. But a word of caution is in order. Do your homework and look for authentic and credible reviews before using a service or software. Automated tools or services that focus on getting you followers, likes, or comments via bots are violating Instagram terms of use. If you give them access to your account, then they are doing it under your name. You could be shadow-banned, or have your account closed. What is being shadow-banned, you ask? It is when Instagram limits your reach, and while your account is technically still active, it is nearly useless. Be warned.

With that said, here is a set of low-cost services and tools that, at the time of this writing, appear to be legitimate, and don't violate Instagram's terms of service. For leveraging your content creatively, try the following:

If This Then That (IFTTT): There is a nice set of recipes using the IFTTT Applet. Learn more about these automated actions here: https://ifttt.com/instagram.

Planmypost: Schedule your posts using Plan My Post. Learn more at https://www.planmypost.com.

For hiring a virtual assistant, consider the following:

FreeeUp: Learn more at www.FreeeUp.com. You can hire pre-vetted freelancers and virtual assistants with experience in Instagram marketing. FreeeUp receives thousands of applicants each week, puts each through an interview and testing process, then takes only the top 1 percent of freelance applicants into the platform.

Popamatic: Hire a virtual assistant to help grow your account for you. Learn more at https://popamatic.com.

Freelancer: Learn more at www.freelancer.com.

Upwork: learn more at www.upwork.com.

Fiverr: Learn more at www.fiverr.com. When searching for services on Fiverr or similar sites, be sure to sort the results by "popularity" to find the most trusted service providers. Look at their total number of reviews—and read them carefully. You do not want to turn your account over to someone who is a novice, or rule-breaker, or both.

When I searched on Fiverr for Instagram services, one name kept coming up—Vasily Kichigin, on Instagram @vasily17 (Figure 8.3). With almost 2,000 authentic five-star reviews and over 12,000 orders completed, his results are undeniable. Vasily has proven he knows what he's doing. His team is solid—and worth looking into as an affordable delegation option. Rather than simply have you wonder about how his services work, I decided to ask him.

Figure 8.3 Vasily Kichigin

**Q&A with Vasily Kichigin—
Fiverr's Top Instagram Service Provider**

Q: How did you get started in an Instagram services business?

A: I started my Instagram business in 2015, before that I was professionally playing tennis and helping my coach with his business of selling fitness mats. I started an Instagram account for his business and was very motivated to develop it and grow the audience. I was learning by doing. In about four months I was able to gain 10,000 followers, and things started to pay off. We got an offer to promote one of our products in *Robb Report* magazine, and after it went live we sold over $45,000 worth. After that experience, I realized that I was super passionate about the process of growing Instagram accounts and decided to come up with a service and offer it on the freelancing platform Fiverr.

Q: How has your business grown?

A: I started freelancing on the side with Instagram marketing at the beginning, since then we've been able to complete over 12,000 orders. It started as a freelance hustle and has turned into a full-time business with more than 15 people working with me.

Q: Who are the typical clients you work with—what are their ambitions and goals?

A: It's a mix. We get about 50 percent business and 50 percent personal accounts. Lots of people with personal accounts want to increase exposure on Instagram. Then we get entrepreneurs running multiple businesses—looking to expand their personal brand on Instagram. We work with a lot of start-ups and even Fortune 500 companies like Marriott. We work with a good number of agencies as well; they outsource our work to their clients.

Q: What do you do for your clients specifically—how does it help scale up their Instagram?

A: We cover everything that needs to be done to have a successful Instagram account. It starts with optimizing an account, making sure all the SEO [search engine optimization] is done right. We work to create relationships with potential customers or followers through engaging with them via messages, comments, following, and liking. We also work on the content creation and management side, making sure each content piece is strategically developed with proper keywords, hashtags, location, and post timing. We work on influencer marketing strategies and running successful Instagram ads.

Q: In your marketing material you assure prospective clients that you help build a following of real, targeted prospects—how do you do that and avoid bots?

A: This is one of the most important goals for us. We do have specific filters applied when we are engaging with users such as making sure the user is consistently posting, and he/she already has a small base of followers and people they follow. Ultimately when we are working with influencers, we are going to each profile and making sure the influencer has excellent engagement. Nowadays the only way to thoroughly analyze the account is actually going and checking the people who liked specific posts and commented on them because the influencer can automate likes, followers, comments, views. We make sure we can fully understand if the profile has real or fake engagement by checking manually to ensure real people are interacting with the posts of that influencer.

Q: What are the typical results customers can expect when they use your service?

A: Before starting a campaign, we set goals with clients. Let's say he/she wants to reach a certain follower number. For example, we have many clients we work with to help them achieve 10,000 followers because at this stage you get the Swipe Up feature in Stories, which is very crucial to make sure you can lead people to your website. With some clients, we have a different approach where we work based on leads and sales. This is more of a long-term strategy and involves running a campaign for longer than three months, for example.

Q: Do you have any clients with extraordinary Instagram success stories?

A: Yes, we do! Unfortunately, I can't disclose the names, but one of the cases we had we were promoting a movie account, and we were able to get over 10,000 followers and build the community of people who were very supportive at the launch. Eventually the movie was a success and the Instagram profile got verified, with a blue badge. We had another case where we built a powerful personal brand for an author and she was able to get featured on CNN News.

Q: Of the clients who don't succeed with you, or don't succeed on Instagram, do you see any common errors or mistakes they make?

A: We do get sporadic cases like that, and they happen because the client is very new to Instagram marketing or they have very unrealistic expectations. My goal is always to overdeliver for the customer. So if we have cases like that, we take more time to explain the concept to the customer, and also showcase different examples and goals that could be achieved. Another typical case is that a client comes to us, and his/her profile has a lot of bot/inactive followers, and they do not realize that at the beginning because someone previously increased their engagement that way. So, in this case, our goal is to make sure we can recover the account and guide the customer on the next actions to take.

Q: For the clients thinking about doing all their Instagram account management themselves, instead of using a service like yours, how much time do you think it would take to match your results?

A: To run a successful Instagram account, you need to treat it as your full-time job. So it's either doing it yourself full-time or finding an expert and letting them do the work. We've already worked with more than 12,000 different Instagram accounts, so we know precisely what actions you need to take.

Q: What encouragement would you give a small-business owner or entrepreneur wanting to grow their business using Instagram?

A. Focus on your content. Don't worry whether you have 10 or 100 followers. Make sure you are producing content daily in your feed and stories. Regularly go live on Instagram. Then, you need to engage with people who leave comments on your posts. That's my top tip. Instagram is all about storytelling and creating a lifestyle with your brand. To successfully do it, you need to start now and document your journey. When you have enough content, and people see the stories behind the account, it is much easier to promote and grow your account.

Q: For readers interested in learning more about your service, where should they connect with you—and do you have any promotional offers you'd like to offer?

A: The best way to find me is through my Instagram @vasily17 or at www.vasilykichigin.com. Mention reading *Instagram Power* and I would be happy to offer you a 20 percent discount on one of our growth packages.

SNAPSHOT

1. Determine how to best automate and delegate, while remaining true to yourself and your audience.

2. Determine to get 1,000 followers as quickly as you can.

3. Spend your time strategically engaging with the right prospects, not just random people.

4. Watch out for negative catalysts for growth and avoid them.

W = WOW THEM WITH EFFECTIVE MARKETING

*Doing business without advertising is
like winking at a girl in the dark.
You know what you are doing,
but nobody else does.*

STUART H. BRITT

Step 9

Master Copywriting Secrets for Instagram

Ultimately you decide your own paycheck. If you're not getting paid enough, become more valuable.

RAY EDWARDS
@rayedwards on Instagram

*a*lthough Instagram is an app for editing and sharing images and video, you still get to do a substantial amount of copywriting. That's great news for those of us trying to promote our brands. As marketers, the challenge of combining words and images will feel very familiar to us. Display advertising is made up of these component parts. It is the skillful use of words and images woven together to tell an interesting story about your product or brand. Yes, we get to do that on Instagram.

So it begs the question: *What would a genius copywriter do if he or she were crafting the written messages associated with an Instagram photo?* Someone like Joe Sugarman comes to mind. Joe is the author of *The Adweek Copywriting Handbook* and is famous for making millions from TV ads featuring BluBlocker sunglasses. How would he use Instagram? Let's first look at the possible writing opportunities and then review how a legendary copywriter might use them.

Writing Opportunities on Instagram

You might be surprised at how many writing elements you can include as you share an Instagram image (see Figure 9.1). Let's review them together.

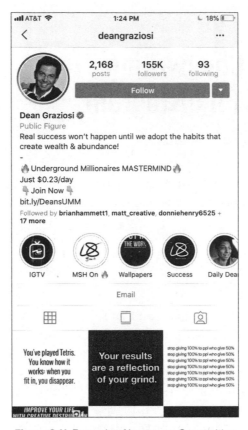

Figure 9.11 Example of Instagram Copywriting

There are two broad categories of writing in Instagram: writing on the image itself and writing that is off the image. Part of the off-image information is referred to as metadata—the information that accompanies the image. But the other part should not be overlooked either, and that includes your profile details. Let's review both the off-image and on-image options.

Off-Image Elements

Smart marketers will use every element of the Instagram system as an opportunity to position their product for success. The strongest presentations will have a seamless flow of information from the off-image elements to the on-image elements. You can use the following off-image locations to share your message:

- **Profile name.** You'll have to decide whether to create an Instagram account for each brand or product line you manage or to create one account that serves your entire company. Obviously the choice will help inform your followers what you're all about. Most large companies that manage multiple brands typically have a unique social media account for each brand. That helps narrow the focus and ensure that you can work with one target market.

- **Comments or responses to comments.** You can add additional information in the comment section. As well, customers can comment, and you can provide additional information as a response.

- **Image caption.** The image caption or description is the primary location for your copywriting. This is where your inner J. Peterman can emerge if you're a product seller. If you're a service seller, this is where you want to position yourself or your service as a solution.

On-Image Elements

Your ability to write on Instagram doesn't stop at the edges of the image. Although the Instagram app's basic functionality doesn't allow you to write on the image, there are many ways to get around this limitation and bring words to life on the image. Once you learn how to add information to your pictures, the opportunities are endless to add descriptions, product names, price information, and other related sales copy. Let's look at a few of the most basic ways to enhance an image with copywriting:

- **Image descriptions or notes.** You can place an informational note or description on the image itself. Depending on the composition of the image, this can easily be added without detracting from the image's focal point. This can be achieved via third-party apps that we'll describe in Step 18.

- **Logo or brand.** You'll have to decide how disciplined you want to be when it comes to adding a brand or logo to your images. In some cases, it makes perfect sense and should be considered. In other cases, it is an unnecessary hassle. Additionally, if you're trying to convey to your followers that you're taking behind-the-scenes shots, then placing a logo or brand mark on your image will not harmonize with that message.

- **Product name.** One aspect of on-image information that can be very helpful to your followers is adding the name of your product to the image. This is particularly true if you have many similar products, like jewelry, shoes, or dresses.

- **Pricing information.** According to the Shopify.com team, Pinterest pins with pricing information receive 36 percent more likes than pins without pricing information. Would that statistic hold true in Instagram? You'll have to test it to find out.

- **Launch date.** As we'll discuss in Step 13, Instagram is an ideal tool for product launches. One of the primary messages for that type of strategy is the announcement of when something will be available. While you can certainly include that information in the off-image description, you can also include it right on the image to reinforce the message.

- **Final sale date.** Scarcity is one of the buying triggers we'll discuss in Step 10. Including a message related to when the doors close or the product stops being sold is a terrific way to help people decide to buy.

How to Get Words on Your Pictures

So what are the best ways to add your messages to images? There are lots of options to choose from. Let's review the most common ways this can be accomplished:

- **Make it in Stories.** The Story Camera gives you a nice range of text and image overlay options. Simply make your image in Stories and then post it to your feed.

- **Third-party apps.** The option to add messages onto your images via third-party apps is endless. These apps generally let you pick an image, write on it, and then save it to your camera's image library, where you can upload it to Instagram. Color Cap, for example, allows you to add text of various colors to an image. There are many other options.

- **Photoshop Elements.** For more complex use of messages on images, you can use Photoshop Elements for the desktop. Don't worry; while the full version of Photoshop might intimidate you, the lighter and simpler Photoshop Elements is made for the novice user. The process for using Photoshop Elements would include editing the image in the program and then placing the image in your camera's library for use on Instagram. There are numerous ways to get an image into your phone's library, the easiest of which is probably to email it to yourself and open the email on your phone.

- **An image of an ad.** You can always simply take a picture of your previously created ad, but this will likely turn out poorly. But sometimes, if it is done in an attractive way, this type of shot can be effective.

- **A screenshot of an ad.** If you have your ad on your website and it looks the way you want it shared on Instagram, then your task is easy. Simply use your smartphone's web browser and take a screenshot. It will take a picture of what you are looking at on your phone and add it to your phone's image library. To take a screenshot on an iPhone 8 or earlier, simply press the Home and Sleep buttons at the same time. For an iPhone with no Home button, simply press and hold the right side button and the up volume button at the same time. Screenshots are possible on Android phones, too. If you are using Android 4.0 (Ice Cream Sandwich) or a later version, then simply hold the Volume Down and Power buttons at the same time.

> **POWER TIP**
> Easily put the images from your website or Facebook photos into your phone's photo album by taking a screenshot of the images you want. Simply navigate to your website, look at the image, and take a screenshot. The image you're looking at will be saved as a picture in your photo album.

Common Myths

There are certainly challenges associated with copywriting for Instagram. Some are real constraints, and some are simply emotional resistance to doing the work, manifested in excuses or inaccurate assumptions. Let's debunk a few of these myths together.

Myth #1: There Isn't Enough Space to Add a Marketing Message

The truth is that all display advertisers are confronted with the challenge of limited space for words. Ever try to write an ad for the side of a bus? How about writing an ad for the top of a taxi? Space is limited in many formats. Dealing with constraints is just part of the creative exercise. In fact, the space restrictions help you hone your message and get very focused. My mantra is "Brevity, Clarity, Content, Style."

Myth #2: Ads Aren't Welcome on Instagram

This is a half-truth that nonmarketers generally wouldn't understand. The reality is that ads are very welcome on Instagram if they are matched to the right audience in the right way and solve a real problem. No one likes advertising when it is unwelcome, but that is like saying no one likes to hear a knock on the door during dinner. If the ad is a perfect solution to your urgent problem, it moves magically into a whole different category in your mind. Suddenly it is not an ad; it is a godsend. The ad becomes a serendipitous moment when your solution materialized just when you needed it most. The knock on the door during dinner isn't unwelcome if it's Publishers Clearing House.

Myth #3: I Will Do More Damage Than Good

If your Instagram followers are made up of your Facebook friends and coworkers, and you try to advertise to them for your new moonlighting career as a multilevel marketer, then you may very well be right. But Instagram won't be any more destructive than your personal emails would be or your unwanted "invitations to dinner." But if you target the right audience on Instagram and cultivate a followership of targeted prospects, then you will be solving problems, not damaging relationships.

Myth #4: Since I Don't Know How to Do Copywriting, I'd Better Not

If you're the marketer for your product or service, then you already know enough to make an effective presentation. Your only challenge is learning how to create effective copy. Luckily, we'll cover that in the next few paragraphs. The good news is that each Instagram image gives you another opportunity to practice this trade skill. Copywriters were not born or somehow ordained when they graduated with an English degree from a university. Copywriters are practitioners who start with a goal and never stop learning how to perfect their craft. You are a perfect candidate.

Myth #5: Social Media Isn't Good for Selling

Sadly, this myth is pervasive and is repeated regardless of which social media site you are talking about. At Pixie Faire, we use YouTube, Facebook, Pinterest, and Instagram to drive sales. Countless other companies use Twitter and Google+. Smart marketers are bonding with prospective customers and leading them through the sales cycle using social media. Don't believe the lie.

Myth #6: You Can't Include Hyperlinks, So Why Bother?

In my first book, I chronicled the amazing power of Pinterest to help marketers build a massive set of referral links within the site that all point toward your website. That puts Pinterest clearly in the category of an Internet marketing gold mine. Yet Instagram has its own strengths and acts much more like traditional offline display advertising. One day, Instagram might allow hyperlinks to be included in image captions. But until then, we can treat it like a fantastic mobile phone display ad system. Nothing wrong with that!

What Would Joe Sugarman Do?

No one would deny that copywriting has an artistic quality to it. But like most well-studied art, there are techniques that emerge over time to become the industry best practices. If you learn the best practices, then you are at least operating within the realm of possible quality. You may still stink at it, but your chances of getting it right improve if you learn the basic lessons.

The best copywriters are masters of technique that they effortlessly weave into their work over years of dedicated practice. They know why they are doing certain things and why they shouldn't do other things. The techniques absorb into their writing to such an extent that it looks intuitive to the outside observer. Thankfully, one of the masters, Joe Sugarman, has documented his work in a copywriting classic, *The Adweek Copywriting Handbook*. Study his work and learn to apply it to Instagram.

The Copywriter's Goal

Think back to a time when you were in a conversation on a topic that didn't interest you in any way. And to add insult to injury, the conversation was with someone you really didn't care to be around. I'd imagine you were trying to be polite, but you really couldn't wait to either change the subject or, ideally, walk away. Now think back to a conversation where someone told you a really exciting piece of gossip. Imagine that on top of it being an amazing piece of news, the person who shared it with you was someone you secretly admired very much and wanted to build a closer relationship with. I bet that you were emotionally engaged, eager to share your perspective, full of questions, and hopeful the conversation wouldn't stop, and that you were smiling and generally hyper. In print and online advertising, the bored walk away—and if they decide they don't like you, they run away. Your job is to position yourself as an interesting person and your product as newsworthy.

If you have your target audience right, then the overall goal of your presentation is to structure the information in a "logical flow" (Sugarman, p. 97) that anticipates the question the viewer might ask next and answers that question. The goal is to start an interesting conversation in the mind of the prospect that the prospect is genuinely enthusiastic about finishing. The goal is getting the attention of the right people and leading them through the process of discovery.

The goal for each element of your presentation should be to strive for engagement with the prospect in this interesting conversation in an appealing way. You don't achieve success by being boring, annoying, or overly spammy in your approach. You achieve success by having a presentation that clicks with your target market and feels very natural, timely, and welcome. As we've outlined, the elements you get to use include the image, the on-image copy, the off-image copy, the metadata elements of your image, and the account-level information.

The Copywriter's View of the Basic Tools

Good copywriters integrate each aspect of the component parts available to create an overall environment. Each component does a job to help shape the environment. Let's look at each of the primary components related to an Instagram image and how a copywriter might consider using them:

1. **The profile name.** To describe who you are in a clear and compelling way. This is an exercise in creative branding that should resonate with your company, product, or personal brand.

2. **The name.** To give you more information and further explain who you are and what you're about. @libertyjaneco becomes Liberty Jane Clothing.

3. **The image.** This is the primary attention-getting device. It has one job to do—capture the attention of the ideal prospect. If it fails to capture the attention of the ideal prospect, nothing else matters.

4. **The on-image writing.** This information, such as a caption, product name, or price, is a critical part of explaining more about the product. It is likely the first written message the prospect will see. It must resonate well.

5. **The image caption.** This is the primary written message that interested prospects will read. It is critically important to continue the conversation and engage the reader by sharing information that helps the reader take the next logical step forward. Where is the item available? When does it go on sale or stop being sold? How much is it? Where can prospects read more information? The description does not need to sound like a sales pitch. It needs to offer answers to top-of-mind questions in a conversational tone.

6. **The comments.** You can immediately leave comments as if they are a "P.S." to offer a bit more information. Or you can wait until someone asks a question. Either way, you have an opportunity to provide additional information about the product or service.

The Copywriter's Outcome

The copywriter is creating an environment that proposes just one logical outcome—buying the product. But it happens in a set of steps. Every time the customer mentally says, *Yes, I like that—tell me more*, the copywriter has done his or her work in that part of the campaign. The overall mood is to have the prospect agree with your presentation, little by little, not in a sneaky or smarmy way, but in an exciting and logical way. The mood should be one of agreement.

On Instagram, that mood can be set. People's interest can be aroused, and their curiosity and enthusiasm can be sparked. The logical next step for selling is to clearly send them to the sales page or e-commerce site. If qualified, enthusiastic prospective buyers go from Instagram to the e-commerce site; then the Instagram marketer's job is done.

Taking Copywriting to the Next Level

In Step 10, we'll continue this conversation and learn about the emotional elements that help create a buying environment and how to include them in the Instagram marketing effort. Let's get started.

SNAPSHOT

1. Copywriting can play a key part in your Instagram marketing work.

2. Evaluate how you can use the on-image and off-image areas to include your messages.

3. The goal of all good copywriting is to get the prospect to take the next logical step.

4. Avoid destructive myths about marketing on Instagram and learn to apply the principles of master copywriters like Joe Sugarman.

Step 10

Use Triggers of Engagement

The most basic human desire is to feel like you belong.
Fitting in is important.

SIMON SINEK
@simonsinek on Instagram

Browse around on Instagram for a few weeks, and you'll notice an interesting trend. People like images that stir them emotionally: vacation destinations, sandy beaches, gourmet cuisine, sunsets, shoes, dresses, pretty places, and pretty faces. People aren't responding to the technical brilliance of an image; they want to be taken on an emotional ride. To see what really strikes a chord, observe people's comments.

In this chapter, we'll dive into the concept of identifying and tapping into these deep-seated emotions and how you can weave them into your Instagram messages to call followers to action in effective ways. If you apply even a hint of these factors in the right way, then positive results will accrue from your work. In some ways, they are like perfume (or cologne)—there is an art to application that makes it not too faint and not too strong.

12 Common Buying Triggers Found on Instagram

There are dozens of emotional triggers that marketers have discovered since direct response marketing began. If you use them in your work, you'll prompt people to act. If you ever have a chance to look at a 1905 Sears Wish Book, a masterpiece of emotional selling, you'll immediately notice the strong use of these types of concepts in the images and copywriting. Instagram provides a new outlet for this age-old method.

For the sake of brevity, let's focus on 12 of the triggers that seem to be particularly prominent in Instagram marketing efforts. These emotional triggers are not mystical, fringe, or quack concepts. Nor are they difficult to figure out. They are completely obvious when you stop to look for them. The challenge for marketers is how to weave them into the story of your product or service in a way that is authentic, honest, and nonmanipulative. The trick is in the implementation. Let's review the 12 factors:

- **Love.** On Instagram, "Love" is a common reply to an image. The message is clear, isn't it? No other information is required. As marketers, we should strive to provide our followers with product images they can love. And if we're service providers, we need to consider how to share a message or concept that people will love. Of course, there is only one thing better than "Love," and that's "Love, Love, Love," which also seems to be a common response. People love places, food, clothing, puppies, and products. They love things they once had long ago, things they have right now, and things they want to get in the future. People are constantly loving something. Of course, the use of the heart emoji stands out nicely in comments.

- **Desire.** Desire comes in many shapes and sizes. People have a deep desire to own things, to meet someone they find attractive, or to be noticed. Part of the sales process is instilling a sense of desire in a prospect, then building that to a higher level, and then helping the person find fulfillment by purchasing the item. We'll demonstrate how to use this trigger in an in-depth way in Step 13.

- **Involvement or ownership.** For most brands, the goal of customer engagement is to build a following of strong advocates who feel a personal involvement in and even ownership of the brand's success. These insiders feel so connected that they have adopted the goal of ensuring your brand is shared far and wide. By using Instagram to give a behind-the-scenes view, you have an opportunity to build a deeper level of involvement.

- **Justifying the purchase.** People need to rationalize a buying decision. People need to have an excuse in order to feel okay about what they've done. The excuse can come in many forms. A 24-hour sale provides an excuse. A coupon provides an excuse. A buy one, get one free (BOGO) offer provides an excuse. A beautiful image of your product provides an excuse for them to like it and share it. Building in a justification that gives prospective buyers an excuse is smart marketing, and it can certainly be done on Instagram.

- **Desire to belong.** For many smaller brands that create a sense of community, the desire to belong can be a powerful emotional trigger. People don't want to feel like they are missing a good party or being left out. Instagram provides a perfect platform to create a sense of belonging and participation.

- **Desire to collect.** Many people collect experiences. As an Instagram user, that is one of the primary activities you'll see being lived out. People collect travel experiences, exotic food experiences, hobby-related experiences, and friendships. People even work to collect followers on Instagram. Is there a way you can help your followers collect things?

- **Curiosity.** One of the strongest emotional triggers for Internet or direct response purchasing is the concept of curiosity. People want to know what the product is like, and they cannot experience it unless they order it. While in a retail environment a product can be picked up, tried on, and felt, in a virtual environment the only solution for strong curiosity is to order the item. Your images can either satisfy people's curiosity or fuel it. Present your items in a way that enhances the mystery and allure instead of squelching it. For example, product images that are zoomed in provide incredible detail, and people immediately think, *I wonder what that fabric feels like?* Good product photography raises more questions than it answers.

- **Storytelling.** The opportunity to reveal a story and include people in a journey is a strong emotional trigger that is available for marketers using Instagram. Do you have a story to tell about your product or service? Can images or videos on Instagram and the associated messages help position your story as intriguing, captivating, and fun?

- **Greed.** What motivates people to hunt for bargains and to swoop in quickly when they see a special deal? Greed is commonly the answer. Greed plays a big part in motivating people to act. Greed motivates people to enter contests, to show up early for a grand opening, and to stay up all night outside a store before a product launch.

- **Urgency.** Having a limited time to respond to an offer creates a sense of urgency. It is one of the best sales tools available. As a marketer, you can introduce a sense of urgency as you create display ads, or you can do it simply by explaining the details of a sale in an Instagram caption.

- **Instant gratification.** Retailers know that the impulse purchase is a key part of their sales opportunity. People want something immediately, and when they are in a buying mood, there is no stopping them. Instant gratification can certainly play a key role in driving consumer behavior on Instagram too. When a new product is launched, the buying mode sweeps over prospects, and they jump into action.

- **Exclusivity.** When something is rare, people inevitably want it more than when it is not. Featuring the rarity or uniqueness of an item tells people that if they want it, they are going to have to act quickly and not delay. They will feel a rush of pride for owning something that is uncommon. Many companies use this strategy intensively as they market items in limited edition sets, for a limited time, or as one-of-a-kind items.

Five Levels of Connection to a Message

Prospects will bond with your photography and messages at different levels. Sometimes you hit a home run—the emotional response to your work is intense and urgent, and a buying decision is easily prompted. Sometimes the level of emotion is not obvious—you only hit a single, and your target market responds mildly to your effort. Sometimes you strike out, and there is no emotional bond formed with your images and associated copywriting. When you do find some success, you are aided by other people's positive sentiments. If people start expressing a positive sentiment about your Instagram images, then you've got allies rallying to your side. You've got a tribe, and the members of your tribe are helping you deliver the message.

There are different levels of resonance people will have with an emotional trigger. Five immediately come to mind. Let's review them in order of weakest to strongest:

1. **They hear it from the company.** The positive sentiment is expressed in the item description or on the image in a way that makes it clear that the company is emotionally "up" about the item. People notice it, but the feeling doesn't transfer to them.

2. **They hear it from a third party.** Seeing a product photo on Instagram and noticing that other people are enthusiastic about it is a higher level of resonance. It is more authentic and powerful to see other people expressing their feelings about something. This is the level at which an Amazon book review resides, for example. This level is relatively easy to obtain on Instagram if you have a following of people who are enthusiastic about your niche or industry.

3. **They hear a weak recommendation from a person they know, like, or trust.** A personal mention of a product or service from someone people know is a fairly powerful emotional

driver. This happens every day when people express a need. Someone will invariably try to be helpful and recommend a product or service, even if he or she hasn't personally tried it. Statements like "I heard so-and-so is pretty good" are common occurrences and provide emotional comfort on several levels. They allow the prospect to have an excuse to buy something, in addition to fueling curiosity.

4. **They say something privately about the company.** The level of emotional engagement goes up dramatically when a prospect is the one expressing the positive sentiment. When a person says, "I want that," even privately, his or her emotions are involved in a way that has a powerful effect on the long-term buying decision.

5. **They say it publicly.** When people are enthusiastic enough about a product or service to put it on their public wish list, then they are engaging emotionally on a very high level. On Instagram, you see people do this frequently, and their positive sentiment is encouraged, reinforced, and seconded by other people. When a group starts collectively saying, "We want this," a virtual frenzy occurs. Look again at the ModCloth image and the 13,200 likes and 353 comments and imagine what that would mean for your product or service.

Fears Related to Tapping into Emotions

If you're feeling uneasy about shaping people's emotional responses, then take a minute and look at the people who are the best in your industry. It really doesn't matter if you're a teacher, insurance salesman, car mechanic, or small retailer. I bet the best people in your industry weave emotion into their work. Do they shape people's emotional responses?

The best teachers are usually good comedians. The best baristas at Starbucks know your name and make you feel included in the community. The best pastors are amazing at telling jokes, parables, and related stories. The best professors raise your level of curiosity to encourage your exploration of the topic. It doesn't matter what industry you are in. You can see these examples every day, in every industry. Hooking people into your work, and then shaping people's emotional responses, is part of influencing them.

> **POWER TIP**
>
> The best communicators in your industry or niche are undoubtedly good at shaping people's emotional responses—from telling stories, to remembering people's names, to using humor. They engage people emotionally and shape their responses.

Your fears about overdoing it are well founded, but you need to develop a comfort level with this idea and figure out how to warm up your work with the power of appropriately used emotional triggers. Let's look at some of the common negative responses to using emotion in selling.

"It Is Manipulative to Play with People's Emotions"

The truth is, we are taught from an early age to influence people by ensuring they are in a good mood when we want to ask for something. Whether it's waiting until your dad is in a good mood to ask for money or bringing your teacher an apple before the big test, we want to use the subtle art of persuasion to ensure that things go our way. But as we learned in kindergarten, it can take forever for some people to get into a good mood on their own, so telling a joke or making them laugh is a way to get them in the right frame of mind before you ask for something. This is no different in the selling context.

"I've Been Burned by This—and Therefore Hate It"

When you've been the victim of any tactic, whether physical, emotional, financial, or psychological, you develop a strong negative opinion and sometimes an aversion to the topic at large. That's perfectly understandable, but that's not a balanced view of things. You don't avoid cars because you were in a wreck, and so you shouldn't avoid using emotion just because someone manipulated yours. If anything, you can use this sensitivity to your advantage and always be sure that you never cross the line.

"No One Loves My Product or Service—It's a Necessary Evil"

If you sell something that no one can get excited about, then it could certainly be the case that social media isn't the right media to use. Maybe direct marketing is better or perhaps a traditional retail strategy. But if you're a service provider, then before you give up so easily, remember that any service can be sold via social media. Because when you sell a service, you are really selling a relationship. People must like you to choose your service. Your ability to cultivate a relationship with a large number of prospective, current, or former clients will directly impact sales.

"I Don't Want to Be Accused of Manipulating People"

If you use the selling triggers in a constructive and upbeat way, there is truly nothing to stress over. If you overdo it or include emotion in a fake way, then you might be accused of being full of too much hype or be seen as a used-car salesman. But chances are, you'll figure out the right balance, and the resulting positive sentiment will start to help you sell.

"I Hate Pressure Tactics"

Everyone hates pressure tactics. But deadlines work to create urgency. Legitimate deadlines will infuse your work with an emotional energy, and if communicated nicely, they won't be seen as a pressure tactic. Pressure tactics are the result of misuse of an emotional approach in a selling context that damages a relationship. They are most frequently used because the seller has urgency due to deadlines, goals, quotas, or other similar motivators. There is no reason to ever use an emotional trigger in a way that breaks a relationship either on Instagram or off.

To get an emotional response from your audience that helps create an upbeat buying mood, you want followers who are truly interested in your product or service. Is it better to have 1,000 true raving fans on Instagram than 10,000 marginally interested fans? I think so! So start with the goal of identifying and serving a core audience. Then share content that they will love. Weave in the other buying triggers as it's appropriate.

SNAPSHOT

1. Learn to identify the common buying triggers and weave them into your work. If you do it well, people will be upbeat and enthusiastic about your efforts.

2. Practice using them in your posts.

3. Learn to identify your own emotional resistance to using selling triggers.

4. The easiest way to get an enthusiastic response to your use of emotional buying triggers is to have followers that are raving fans. Take the time to build your followers strategically so it's not an uphill battle.

Run Contests and Use Freebies Regularly

Winning is only half of it.
Having fun is the other half.

BUM PHILLIPS

Contests work great on Instagram. Random giveaways and long-term free promotional products work great too. From free samples at Costco to free Kindle e-books on Amazon, people love free things. So let's give it to them. If you want to sell a lot of products or services, learn to leverage the power of free. In this chapter, we'll share ideas and tips for using the power of free. If you have products, you have an opportunity to use the power of free; and if you're a service provider with no product to offer, keep reading—this chapter is for you, too. The power of free can be leveraged for service businesses just as easily as for product-focused businesses.

How to Get 64 Times More Comments

According to research by Tailwind, Instagram accounts that hold contests grow 70 percent faster than those that don't. Tailwind found that contest posts get 64 times the comments compared to normal posts. In fact, it reports that 91 percent of Instagram posts with over 1,000 comments are contests. Want even more engagement than that? It reports that holding a contest with another brand raises the engagement by another 79 percent compared to contests that are done alone.

And Yet, It's So Uncommon

Is every business running contests on Instagram? Not even close. According to the Tailwind research, only 2 percent of Instagram accounts conduct contests—and the majority of those do it only intermittently. So creative marketers have a huge opportunity to use contests to build their tribe. In his classic book *Free: The Future of a Radical Price*, Chris Anderson explains how innovative companies are using free as a competitive tool:

> *Companies look at a portfolio of products and price some at zero (or close to it) to make other products, on which they make healthy profits, more attractive. Technology is giving companies greater flexibility in how broadly they define their markets, allowing more freedom to give away some products to promote others.*

Why You Should Give a Free Item Instead of a Coupon

Using free items is a strategy that can work very effectively, as an alternative to simply running sales constantly to try to generate business. I realize many businesses use coupons and do it effectively. So there is a place for it. But in my view, when you run sales and simply discount your prices, you are doing the following:

1. You are putting your customers in a chronic state of waiting for the "next big sale."

2. The message you are sending when you put your work on sale is that the "true worth" is less than the originally stated price.

3. Coupons and discounts work like a drug in your sales system. Yes, you can become addicted to coupons. Coupons give you an

unrealistic boost of everything: customer traffic, enthusiasm, and sales. But the effect wears off quickly, and you want to do it again.

4. By selling a large portion of your inventory or service at a lower-than-desired price, you erode profit margins.

5. Coupons suppress creativity. Coupons and sales are easy, and when you do them, you don't work to find the harder, more interesting customer engagement activities that can produce similar results.

Effective Contest Strategies on Instagram

There are many types of contests, and you'll want to consider how best to conduct one to support your brand. You might want to frequently search the phrase "creative Instagram contests" to see what exciting strategies fellow marketers are coming up with. Here are several that I've seen work well. Of course, the big question in your mind might be, are contests allowed on Instagram? The short answer is yes. I'd encourage you to visit the promotion guidelines in Instagram's help center. Simply google Instagram Promotion Guidelines, or visit the link here: https://help.instagram.com/179379842258600. Let's explore a few common types of contests.

"Name It to Win It" contest. The ModCloth "Name It and Win It" contest is a good example of an easy-to-achieve Instagram contest. It generated thousands of comments. The reason we like this contest model is because the entry method is right on the image. There is no secondary site involved and no hashtag. This maximizes participation and allows people to jump in quickly.

Comment contest. A very simple Instagram contest is the comment contest. The trick with this type of contest is to use it creatively to engage your tribe, get them sharing, or get them to reveal their interests or opinions so you can be a better marketer. For example, if you sell vintage clothing, but you're not sure what is most popular with your audience, you could ask people to answer a question related to their favorite fashion style from the sixties. You get the idea—tie the comment to actionable marketing insights.

"Like to Win" contest—The simplest of all Instagram contests is the "Like to Win" contest. This will help with engagement, too, which is always a good thing. Simply create a prize and let your tribe know the winner will be chosen at random from the people who like the post.

"Repost to Win" contest—Have an image you want replicated hundreds or thousands of times? Create a "Repost to Win" contest. Of course, the image you have participants repost will need to have some on-image messaging so your marketing message is carried forward by your participants as they repost it.

Multiple entry contests—Another, broader contest strategy is one we run every week at our e-commerce site, Pixie Faire. We call it our Mod Doll Monday contest, and to achieve it we use an embedded RaffleCopter widget (http://www.rafflecopter.com) on a blog post. You can have multiple entry methods. Common entry methods include sign-up for our newsletter, follow us on Instagram, Like an Image on Instagram, follow us on Pinterest, Like a Pinterest Image, etc. Entry methods can vary from week to week so people don't get bored with it. While some entry methods can be completed only one time, such as sign-up for our newsletter, other options, like having people comment on your newest Instagram image or video, or repin a new Pinterest Pin, can be done in an ongoing way, and it never gets old. You'll notice that in Figure 11.1 we had 29,477 entries.

Best Practices for Contest Legal Disclosures

Contests are serious business. They are regulated by the platforms you use, such as Instagram, Facebook, and Pinterest, as well as by state laws, and finally by the federal government in the United States. In other countries around the world, similar legal oversight is in place as well. Always be sure to research how each layer of oversight impacts you and operate professionally and ethically. Although I'm not an attorney, here are some best practices that are commonly shared online.

Figure 11.1 Multiple Entry Contest

☐ Comply with Instagram's Promotion Guidelines, found in its help center. In particular, you cannot encourage users to tag someone in their content who is not actually in the photo they've shared. Instagram sees this as a form of spam. You should also include a phrase such as, "By entering you acknowledge this promotion is in no way sponsored, endorsed or administered by, or associated with, Instagram" and release them of liability.

☐ Comply with state and federal laws.

☐ Use the "No purchase necessary" phrase. This ensures you're not running an illegal lottery, which is against the law.

☐ Have official rules posted online that describe the details of the promotion. For example, is it a sweepstakes, aka giveaway, where wining is based solely on random chance? Or is it a skills-based contest with some criteria for entry?

☐ Have a public start date and end date.

☐ Have age and residency restrictions. Use the "Void Where Prohibited" phrase. This lets people know that anywhere your contest is illegal, they are ineligible to win. Generally participants need to be 18 years or older.

☐ Encourage anyone entering via a public statement on social media to disclose they are "posting for a chance to win a prize." That ensures their followers know their post is part of a promotion.

Expansion Pack Gift—Three Hours of Contest Training

One of my bestselling courses on Udemy is called Social Contests Blueprints. It's a deep dive into how my Inner Circle and coaching students are using contest strategies effectively. I'm happy to give you free access as a reader exclusive bonus. Again, get the Expansion Pack at www.winning.online.

Beyond Contests

Giving away one of your products, or a service, is a great way to get attention. You don't always have to run a contest to do it. There are countless variations on this theme, and you'll have to decide how it works best for your business, but it does work to energize prospective as well as existing customers. You could simply give free shipping for a limited time. Look at how Alphabet Bags, @alphabetbags on Instagram does it (Figure 11.2).

Free Digital Products

When traditional businesses integrate a collection of free digital products into their business model, they can see substantial benefits. In this approach, rather than using free as a short-term gimmick to get interest and attention, the marketer takes free to a much deeper level and allows customers to get something of real value in exchange for something that is nonmonetary, like an email opt-in.

Figure 11.2 Free Shipping Promo

While this method of prospect engagement has been around for many years, people who are referred to as Internet marketers pioneered this business model in its digital form. The benefits associated with the practice are clear and easy to evaluate. A free product line, if done right, attracts the attention of your ideal customers and gets them into a relationship with you. It also acts as an ethical bribe to get the customer to act in beneficial ways. Give away a free e-book on a related topic in order to get the customer's email address.

The Stealthy Way to Share Boring Content

As Mary Poppins joyfully sang, a spoonful of sugar makes the medicine go down. When you give something away for free, like a how-to guide, you have the opportunity to include valuable but hard-to-convey information. Things such as:

1. Your company's mission, vision, and values.

2. Your founding story.

3. Your product's unique selling proposition and reason for existence.

4. Your philosophical approach to your product or craft.

5. Upselling and cross-selling explanations—how your products all fit together to serve the customer.

6. Your seasonality, annual cycle of production or design, and product design process.

7. Your customer service approach, methods, and practices.

8. Your commitment to your product or service and guarantee of satisfaction or happiness—in other words, a longer explanation of your guarantee.

9. Your future plans and upcoming projects. Sharing what you're going to do next allows prospective customers to buy into your vision and get excited about what you're going to do.

Ritualize the Freebies for Maximum Impact

A ritual of sharing something free at a set interval is one of the most powerful marketing tactics you can introduce. On our e-commerce site, Pixie Faire, we give away a free PDF guidebook every Friday—each Friday, it's a different one. The methodology helps prospects and customers come to appreciate visiting the website every Friday. On any given Friday we'll have between 10,000 and 13,000 copies downloaded.

This system could work monthly or even annually, such as offering a free e-book each January. Or, as Jeff Walker does, offering a free workshop every year as part of his product launch. More on how to apply his strategy in Step 13. In our case, since we have a catalog of over 2,400 PDFs, and our customers end up purchasing many of them, offering them one free each Friday in exchange for coming to visit our site isn't that big a deal. Of course, when they visit, they also shop. It probably wouldn't surprise you to learn that Friday is our biggest selling day of the week.

SNAPSHOT

1. You can use the power of free on Instagram to build your brand.

2. Set a date to launch a contest on Instagram and see how it resonates with your target market.

3. Create a helpful free product and begin advertising it on Instagram.

4. Get the free three-hour Social Contests Training in the Expansion Pack at www.winning.online.

Selling Directly on Instagram

*Selling stuff is easy. All you gotta do is give away
stuff that makes people happy . . . and then sell
them stuff that makes them even happier.*

FRANK KERN
@frankkern on Instagram

nstagram is a fantastic place to sell products. We talked, in
the last chapter, about how running contests or giving away
a free product can serve as a great preselling effort to acquire
new prospects. But that's not enough. It's time to sell directly on
Instagram.

In this chapter, we'll look at direct selling options using the
Shoppable Tags feature as well as a tried-and-true form of old-school
display advertising, which anyone can use and is also free. Then, in
upcoming chapters, we'll dive into the Instagram Advertising program options and learn how paid advertising on the platform can help
sell what you've got.

When you put it all together, you begin to realize that Instagram
has a powerful set of selling tools that any marketer can use regardless of whether you are a physical product seller, services seller, local
merchant, consumer brand, or nonprofit. Instagram has executed
brilliantly on update after update over the years, giving us marketers
the tools we need to sell. Let's jump in.

Shoppable Tags

In 2016 Instagram unveiled the Shoppable Tags feature for image posts, aka Shoppable Posts. As of 2018, they are testing it in Stories too. The feature allows approved merchants to add up to 5 tags to an image, or 20 to a carousel, with active links taking browsers directly to the product (see Figure 12.1) with the Instagram feed. It also gives access to the Shoppable Posts via a Shop button on the business account profile. These features are an absolute game-changer for sellers that qualify to use them.

Who Qualifies to Use Shoppable Tags

Unfortunately, the feature is only available to a specific group of business account holders—the qualifications are listed below. But if we've learned anything about Instagram, it's that it will likely expand and improve this functionality in the future. For example, currently you cannot pay to promote a Shoppable Post, but it seems logical for that functionality to exist in the near term. If and when it does, it will add rocket fuel to this blazing e-commerce fire.

To learn more about the current program details and guidelines, and see the latest updates, be sure to visit the Instagram Business Tools section of the Help Center at: https://help.instagram.com. You can also find blog articles and tips at https://business.instagram.com /a/shopping-on-instagram. Here is an overview of the qualifications at the time of this writing.

- ☐ First, you must be using a Business Profile, apply to be an approved seller, and sell items that comply with Instagram's Merchant Agreement and commerce policies.
- ☐ Country locations seem to be expanding quickly, but currently they're limited to United States, Argentina, Australia, Austria, Belgium, Belize, Brazil, Bulgaria, Canada, Croatia, Cyprus, Czech Republic, Denmark, Dominican Republic, Ecuador, Finland, France, Germany, Greece, Hungary, Ireland, Italy, Korea, Latvia, Lithuania, Luxembourg, Malta, Mexico, Netherlands, New Zealand, Norway, Panama, Paraguay, Peru, Poland, Portugal, Puerto Rico, Romania, Slovenia, South Africa, Spain, Sweden, Switzerland, and Uruguay.

Figure 12.1 Shoppable Tags

☐ You must create a Shop Catalog on Facebook. You can make it either directly on your Facebook page or via the Facebook Business Manager.

☐ For Shopify and BigCommerce users, you can enable Facebook and Instagram as a sales channel to enable this functionality.

Being a Shopify user for our e-commerce work at Pixie Faire, when I first heard about Shoppable Posts, I was ecstatic. Billionaire time. But when I discovered that we didn't qualify because our catalog is all digital goods, I was bummed. If you feel the same way, don't worry, there are other methods that we can use. Are they as cool as Shoppable Posts, no. But, as Bruce Lee once said, "Use only that which works, and take it from any place you can find it." Let's look at what works for everyone on Instagram.

Third-Party Alternative to Shoppable Tags

There are alternatives to the Shoppable Tags feature. The leader is Curalate. It leverages the link in the account bio to build a replica of your Instagram feed and provides the opportunity for visitors to purchase items from your website. Although the user experience isn't as seamless as the official Shoppable Tags feature, it's worth investigating. Check out Curalate at www.curalate.com. Browse to its case study section at https://www.curalate.com/resources/#success and look at the examples. Anytime you see the link in the bio that includes "like2b.uy/[storename]," you know it's powered by Curalate. To see several accounts that use Curalate, look at @hobbylobby, @lulus, @raymourflanigan, or @jcrew (Figure 12.2).

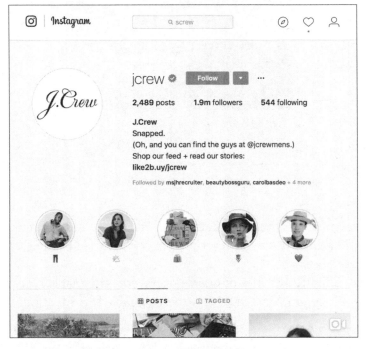

Figure 12.2 J.Crew with like2b.uy/jcrew Link

Traditional Display Ads Adapted to Instagram

When you put product photography and clever copywriting together, you have a classic form of display advertising. This type of marketing works well on Instagram, it's free, and it has been perfected over the last century. Early pioneers in direct response marketing created the Sears Wish Book and other early forms of direct mail catalogs. The Sears catalog was a massive advertising book that included product images and copywriting for an incredible number of products. Instagram is the modern day equivalent.

The basic concepts associated with display ads haven't changed very much in over a hundred years. Some of the earliest examples are from catalogs; then the practice expanded to billboards, magazines, and newspapers and eventually moved online. There are even display ads in virtual worlds such as Second Life.

This form of advertising works on Instagram really well. It seems that some things never go out of style. In his incredible book on advertising, *Hey Whipple, Squeeze This*, Luke Sullivan notes that "the crafts of copywriting and art direction, [are] two disciplines that are infinitely portable. Everything you learn about writing and art direction here applies to pretty much every surface you're working on, from bus sides to computer screens" (p. 36).

So when your CEO asks if you have a comprehensive marketing campaign figured out for Instagram, you get to say, "Yes, we do— we are adapting our best display ads to that format and testing response."

So how do you adapt your best display ads for Instagram? Or how do you create them effectively if you aren't familiar with this process? Let's explore those questions together in this chapter.

What Does Your Tribe Think Is Visually On-Trend?

There is an unspoken rule in display ad marketing that I'm about to share. Here it is: you can get away with being very direct in your message—as long as your target market thinks the message and photo are trendy. Marketers call this being on-trend. But if the prospects in your target market feel like they're being sold something in an uncool way, prepare to be ignored, unfriended, or even publicly called out. It can get ugly out there.

What's cool, aka on-trend, for your target market? It will look very different from industry to industry. It will be different for male versus female demographics. It changes over time, and probably the biggest stylistic differences will have to do with the age of your target market. Learn to identify what works visually for your niche and adapt it to your work.

Display Ad Techniques

Display ad methods vary over time, and styles are influenced by many factors, including:

- Culture
- Photography techniques
- Language and grammar
- Technology

But there are commonsense guidelines and basic principles that you can start using today. You don't need to be a professional marketer to use these techniques. Let's look at the basic ideas.

Concept #1: People Like Their Likeness

One thing that is common sense to most marketers is that people like seeing images of people in their demographic. They like their own likeness, and seeing ads that have people they can relate to helps them receive the message. Ads working to cultivate 18- to 24-year-olds need to use product photography that shows 18- to 24-year-olds. So the Hollister ads show 18-year-olds without their shirts on. And the Mop & Glo ads show 35-year-old women happily mopping. Again, you probably already knew this; most people do. The only question is, *Can you weave age-appropriate likeness into your Instagram work?*

Concept #2: Humor Works Better Than Fact

If you have the opportunity to weave humor into your ad, you'll do yourself a huge favor. Humor lightens the mood, disarms the antagonistic, and sets the stage for a positive interaction.

Concept #3: Curiosity Prompts Action

The best display ads pique the interest of people so much that they take the initiative to track down further information. Traditional outdoor display ads or print ads had a huge barrier between interest and action. Prospects would have to find a phone and call a number or send away for more information, or in more recent times, they could visit a website or send an email. Old-school marketers learned that developing a very strong sense of curiosity was important, and they found that including strong calls to action that centered on some type of urgency was best. Limited-time offers, fast-action bonuses, and similar devices are all used to overcome the "I'll do it later" mentality.

To some extent, this same barrier exists on Instagram, but at least the interested consumers are just one click away from getting a link to your website. They simply click on your user profile and click through to the link for your website. Many Instagram advertisers are learning that the old-school techniques still work. The curiosity must be intense, and the call to action clear and urgent.

Concept #4: Showing Is Better Than Telling

Can you use the image in your ad to make a point rather than stating it in the copy? Showing is better than telling, and if you can use photography creatively, your ad will be well received.

At the same time, the image should complement the message, not simply repeat it. There are two tracks to run on when you're creating a display ad, and you should work to optimize both. First, there is the visual concept that includes the image and any on-image copywriting, and then there is the written concept both on the image and off the image. You want to make sure you use both tracks creatively.

Concept #5: Never Be Boring

There are a million and one ways to be boring. Overcoming that common pitfall is hard work. How do you do it? First, you have to work to transcend mediocrity in the image selection process. Second, you have to come up with a crisp and authentic approach to the writing. Finally, you have to break through the noise and clutter of Instagram to get noticed.

Concept #6: Get Interesting Visuals from Your Product Photography

Your product has a typical way of being photographed that your customers and prospects are probably very used to seeing. Then there are more artistic approaches—try your best to find those. An interesting image holds people's attention. Layer on an interesting message about the image, and you have the opportunity to engage with prospects in a powerful way.

Concept #7: Avoid Clichés

Every niche or industry has common photos, graphics, and image concepts that are overused. Worse, there are tired words, phrases, and statements that have lost their impact and snap. When you combine predictable imagery with cliché wording, you get a super-boring ad that not only will fail to capture anyone's attention but will also position you as irrelevant, outdated, and uninspired. You don't want to be that marketer; you don't want to be that company.

Concept #8: Simplify

The most powerful ads focus on one messaging goal, and they crush it. Their simplicity is their strength. Rather than trying to accomplish a handful of objectives, you'll need to sacrifice, reduce, boil down, and chop. You'll need to make your image and copy so simple that the concept is fully communicated at first glance.

Remember—Image, Then Words

Find a great image and build a story around it. Sometimes an image calls for a certain type of commentary. There is no better way to build an ad than to get a powerful picture of your product, company, or concept and then create an ad concept that expands on the idea that is already inherent in the image.

How to Close the Sale with Link in Bio

One of the biggest challenges with Instagram is the limited opportunity to share active links. Many marketers simply use the link in their bio in support of their current campaign, changing it every time they have a post that focuses on something new. Then, in the caption of their post or video, they say, "see link in bio." But that's limiting, and each of your prior posts will be outdated after you change the link in your bio. Although it's not a perfect solution, you can expand the opportunity to share links in your bio by using one of the many bio link expanding tools such as:

- Linktree: www.linktr.ee
- LNK.Bio: www.lnk.bio
- Tap Bio: www.tap.bio

SNAPSHOT

1. Instagram enables direct selling in several ways.

2. Start with a powerful image and define the message to complement it.

3. The message must be simple and direct.

4. Use the link in your bio to expand your selling options.

Use Multistep Campaigns and User Generated Content

*The next wave of the Web is going
to be user generated content.*

JOHN DOERR

There are several other campaign styles that many marketers are using very effectively on Instagram. Some are new
to Instagram, and some are adaptations from strategies that
have worked for decades. I refer to these as "multistep" campaigns
because they involve multiple steps. Although the topic of user generated content, UGC, probably deserves its own chapter, and maybe
its own book, I've included it here.

The reason a multistep campaign is so powerful is because it gives
the marketer multiple opportunities to talk about something in a low-
pressure, authentic, and casual way. The art of a multistep campaign
is the unveiling of details or messages over an extended period of
time. Through several posts of different content varieties, the marketer works to capture attention, pique interest, create a desire to buy,
and then give a call to action. When you add multiple voices to the
campaign, via user generated content and influencer marketing strategies, these campaigns take on a life of their own.

The opposite of a multistep campaign is a hard sell, one-and-done post, which most marketers feel awkward about publishing, and most followers don't want to see. You don't need to do that to sell things on Instagram.

When you add multistep strategies to your own Instagram Content Blueprint efforts and Daily Actions, you're going to add real leverage to your marketing efforts. Let's explore the use of multistep campaigns, then look at specific applications you can use on Instagram today.

The Dawn of the Multistep Campaign

These steps aren't new to most marketers; they are known as the classic AIDA marketing formula (attention, interest, desire, action). It is the basis for most marketing campaigns today.

Although AIDA isn't new, the journey of how it started is worth understanding. From the print advertising world of 1899, to the direct response marketers of the 1950s, to the Internet marketers of the 1990s, to the Instagram marketers of today, AIDA has stood the test of time and been adapted to many different forms. Its application to Instagram marketing is another step in its evolution.

The Origin of AIDA

A catalog marketer named Fred Macey first wrote about the four-step plan that has become known as AIDA in 1899. That year, the Bissell carpet sweeper company held a contest and asked Macey to be the expert judge. The contest was to see who could make the best advertisement for Bissell's carpet-cleaning machines. Macey's guidelines were described as follows:

> *1st. The advertisement must receive "Attention," 2d. Having attention it must create "Interest," 3d. Having the reader's interest it must create "Desire to Buy," 4th. Having created the desire to buy it should help "Decision." ("The Bissell Prize Advertisement Contest,"* Hardware, *March 1900, p. 44, from Wikipedia)*

The AIDA Model Gets on the *Not-So-Super* Highway

In Minneapolis in 1925, the Burma-Shave company started using roadside signs to sell its product—shaving cream. The signs became a hallmark of outdoor display advertising in the early years of the American highway system, when cars were still relatively slow. The Burma-Shave signs were developed to contain six brief messages, each message on a different sign. As drivers would pass them, the full message of the campaign would be revealed. The sign campaigns ran successfully from 1925 through 1962. An example of the sign messages is as follows:

> *Our fortune*
> *Is your*
> *Shaven face*
> *It's our best*
> *Advertising space*
> *Burma-Shave*

As roads improved and speeds increased, it became a less effective way to use the AIDA model. But the concept of using AIDA in a multi-message serial way was born. The breakthrough was that you could break the AIDA model into multiple messages and share them over time. Although the roadside signs ended, AIDA moved on to new platforms.

The AIDA Model Goes Postal

Direct mail marketers became very accustomed to using the AIDA model. Direct mail, it seemed, was a natural way to apply the method. The best direct response marketers and agencies perfected the model through constant testing and refinement. Over time, they learned that advertisements that were longer, with lots of copy and product information, were better than shorter-form ads. Through the long-form letter, you have the chance to fully develop each of the elements of the AIDA model. The customer gets engaged, convinced, and, through involvement, sold.

The AIDA Model Finds the Super Highway

By the 1990s the AIDA model was very common in all forms of direct response marketing. It worked in display ads in newspapers and magazines, outdoor display ads, direct mail, and television, and it was about to find its way onto the Internet.

Internet marketers realized that capturing email addresses and sending prospects a series of messages to generate a sale was yet another version of the model. The system, still very much used today, includes two steps. First, the marketer captures the email address from a prospect in the targeted niche or industry, and then in subsequent email messages the marketer uses the AIDA model to sell all sorts of related products in that niche.

Jeff Walker's Breakthrough Adaptation

Jeff Walker (on Instagram @jeffwalkerco) is a Colorado-based Internet marketer, widely regarded as a pioneer in adapting the AIDA model to the task of launching a product on the Internet in a serial way. I'd highly recommend his book and course to you. His book *Launch: An Internet Millionaire's Secret Formula to Sell Almost Anything Online, Build a Business You Love, and Live the Life of Your Dreams*, outlines his process. Jeff started his journey toward becoming the launch guru by writing a stock market newsletter. He wanted a way to engage prospective customers, with the hope of signing them up for his monthly paid subscription. Starting with a very small list, and with the AIDA model in serial form adapted to the Internet, he built a six-figure business in six days. His use of the model worked.

He first used emails as the method to share the AIDA content as separate but related messages. Later, he pioneered the use of videos to engage with prospective customers. His approach was to break the long-form sales letter into a series of unique messages, each building toward the launch of the product. He called it the "sideways sales letter." It was the AIDA model in a serial format, à la Burma-Shave signs, applied to an information product launch.

Jeff has helped literally thousands of marketers adapt this model to their products—including Cinnamon and me. We are honored to be a featured case study in his launch materials. Our first use of his model was in support of our Design Academy program. We were shocked at how effective it was in radically increasing our sales. We've been a huge fan of his work ever since.

Jeff's Ten Pre-Prelaunch Questions

In this terrific book, Jeff offers ten pre-prelaunch questions that are smart for any marketer to consider before starting a campaign, regardless of whether you're working on another platform or on Instagram. They are:

1. How can I let people know something is coming without having it feel like I'm trying to sell them something?

2. How can I tease their curiosity?

3. How can I get their help in creating this product—and make it collaborative?

4. How can I figure out what their objections are to this product?

5. How can I start to engage my prospects in a conversation about my offer? How can I be engaging and avoid the corporate speak that will kill my launch before it starts?

6. How can I make this fun and humorous and even exciting?

7. How can I stand out in a crowded market? How can I be different?

8. How can I figure out how my market wants to be sold?

9. How can I figure out my exact offer?

10. How can this naturally lead into my prelaunch sequence?

The AIDA Model on Instagram

As you might guess, the AIDA model has found its way onto Instagram. Multipart messages are fun and entertaining. Creative marketers are using them to count down to big events, product launches, and sales events. Layering on user generated content and influencer marketing adds fuel to the fire. Figure 13.1 shows an example of a multistep announcement from Jessica Alba's company, The Honest Company, @honest on Instagram.

Figure 13.1 Multistep Announcement

Your ability to adapt this approach is endless. Look to see how other Instagrammers are doing it and adapt things to your situation. Break the message up, make it engaging, and have fun. Let's look at some popular multistep campaigns—some we've already talked about, and some we'll share in greater detail here.

- **The countdown-to-reveal campaign.** As mentioned in Step 4, a countdown-to-reveal campaign is straightforward and can be used by any type of Instagram marketer. Use it as part of your prelaunch strategy.

- **The contest campaign.** As mentioned in Step 11, contests create a fantastic multipart campaign option. The trick is to be sure they are tied to some type of product or service call to action. Be sure to run your contests for a reason and use them to close the deal.

- **The Instagram photo challenge.** We'll outline this fun multistep campaign in greater detail as the final suggestion in this chapter. Use it to get people talking, and guide the conversation toward your brand and products.

- **The user generated content campaign.** Building an ongoing mechanism to adopt user generated content is the ultimate multistep campaign. You sell a product, ask customers to share about it using a hashtag, then repurpose their content for additional marketing efforts. More about how to do this in the next few chapters.

- **The bio link to landing page campaign.** The simplest multi-step campaign is to use the link in your bio to take visitors to a landing page where you invite them further into your funnel. Offer a webinar, a free report, an invitation to join your newsletter list, etc.

- **Free gift via bio link to ManyChat enrollment.** Some smart marketers are using the bio link to offer a free gift. When clicked upon it takes you to a ManyChat Facebook Messenger tool. When you "opt-in" to that tool, you're placed on the marketer's ManyChat list. If you're not familiar, Many-Chat (wwwmanychat.com) is a tool for building a Facebook Messenger opt-in list that you can then send messages to in a broadcast format.

- **Bio link to landing page that is pixeled for retargeting.** By using your post caption to encourage your Instagram followers to click the link in your bio, and when they do, they are sent to a page where you have a Facebook pixel installed, it gives you the opportunity to run retargeting campaigns to the visitors. Of course, you don't have to be the one directly retargeting them to benefit from this strategy. You'll notice that in my bio link @mrjasonmiles, I frequently have a link and call to action encouraging people to go to my Udemy courses. Why would I send them to Udemy instead of my own site? Because Udemy runs retargeting ads very aggressively. In essence, it pays for the retargeting campaigns that prompt people to buy my courses. When it works, my Udemy sales go up, pushing my courses up the Udemy organic rankings, which drives even more sales.

Marketing with User Generated Content

If your tribe is producing content in connection with your contests, products, services, or events, then your goal should be to figure out how best to use it to influence others. There are lots of exciting options. Let's explore them.

Feature User Generated Content on Your Website

One simply way to leverage the power of user generated content is by adding it to your website. The tools to do this and the functionality they offer will vary depending on how your site is built. While I can't cover all options for all e-commerce sites here, I'd encourage you to search the web for solutions for your particular situation. For Shopify sites owners, try:

- **The Covet app:** https://apps.shopify.com/covet-pics

- **TagTray:** https://www.tagtray.com

For WordPress site owners, try:

- **Instashow:** https://elfsight.com/instagram-feed-instashow/

- **Instagram Feed:** https:// wordpress.org/plugins/instagram-feed/

Example UGC on Pixie Faire

We run our e-commerce site, Pixie Faire, on Shopify, so we use the Covet app. It works brilliantly. The app allows us to create image layouts in different configurations. For example, on the bottom of our homepage we have a carousel of UGC, and a call to action to visit our "Inspiration Page." The inspiration page uses a Covet configuration that looks like a Pinterest style grid that scrolls down the page a good way (see Figure 13.2).

Figure 13.2 Pixie Faire Inspiration Page

Each image featured is moderated, so we only add what we want to our site, and is also linked to corresponding products available on our site, so visitors can click on an inspiration image in the gallery and quickly buy the associated products (Figure 13.3).

Figure 13.3 Links to Products

How this content gets identified and then added to the site happens in one of two ways. The Instagrammer either tags our username or uploads the content straight to the Covet app by following the directions on our site. It is then moderated, products are linked, and it is made visible on the site.

Repost the UGC on Your Own Instagram Profile—with Approval

It used to be against the Instagram terms of service to post content that you did not own, but Instagram has softened its stance and now allows you to do it. So it's now a common practice for brands to repost UGC or other people's content with attribution. To do it professionally, take the following steps:

1. Ask permission via a comment on the original post or via DM. Only post if you get it. If the user has conditions, or asks for a cash payment, work out the details.

2. When working with influencers who are posting on your behalf, be sure to include a copyright waiver in your contracts so you have standing permission to repurpose the content.

3. Use a repost app, such as Instarepost, www.instarepostapp.com, or Repost, www.repostapp.com, or simply take a screenshot of the original and share it.

4. Use the word "regram" or the hashtag #RG in your post caption to clarify that it is being shared from someone else. Then give credit to the original content creator in the caption of the post by tagging the user, for example @mrjasonmiles.

Create a Photo Challenge

An Instagram Photo Challenge can take a lot of forms and is a fun activity that gets people engaged. Some challenges have gone viral. For example the #hobbylobbychallenge, which Hobby Lobby didn't engineer but is benefiting from, has teen girls going to do a photo in the floral section of Hobby Lobby. With over 31,000 uses of the hashtag, it's turned into a fun ongoing activity.

A more structured approach many marketers are taking is to create a photo prompt for each day that spans a certain amount of time. In that way, you create the rules of the game. In a recent post on her website, podcaster and business coach Melyssa Griffin, on Instagram @melyssa_griffin, shared her experience and tips in seven steps. You can read the full article at: https://www.melyssagriffin.com/hosting-instagram-challenge/. Her tips include:

1. Partner up with other Instagrammers.
2. Select a good hashtag for your challenge.
3. Keep your prompts simple—for example "yellow."
4. Select a manageable length of time—two weeks for example.
5. Directly invite people (your tribe) to join before it starts.
6. Interact with participants.
7. Do a recap on your blog.

To do a deep dive into Instagram challenges and how to do them well, check out the article "Best Instagram Challenges for Makers and Why You Should Be Taking Part" by Folksy.com at https://blog.folksy.com/2017/06/07/best-instagram-challenges. I've included mention of a few below. Some Instagrammers get so passionate about this method that they create entire accounts dedicated to the idea. Others add the concept to a blog post or social post and share it widely. Here are some examples to get you up and running:

- It's My Week—@its_my_week.
- Hobby Lobby Challenge—#hobbylobbychallenge.
- Weekend Hashtag Project—run by Instagram and shared every week on its Facebook page. See how it works at https://www.facebook.com/instagram/.
- A Quiet Style—run by Emma Harris @aquietstyle and reposted @_aquietstyle.
- The Hundred Day Project—the100dayproject.org, run by @elleluna and @lindsayjeanthomson.
- Floral Week Friday—Run by @emilyquinton, #floralweekfriday.

SNAPSHOT

1. Learn to use the AIDA model on Instagram to instill a sense of enthusiasm for your products.

2. Master the creative use of user generated content (UGC) on Instagram.

3. Add UGC to your site and use it effectively to encourage purchasing.

E = EXPAND WITH ADVERTISING AND INFLUENCERS

*The essence of influence is pull.
It's an attraction. Great influencers attract people,
to themselves, and to their ideas.*

BOB BURG

Start Advertising on Instagram

*What really decides consumers to buy
or not to buy is the content of
your advertising, not its form.*

DAVID OGILVY

t's time to add fuel to your bonfire with paid advertising. In this chapter, we'll review the Instagram advertising options, look at best practices, and get you up and running like a pro. And if, by chance, you want to hand the tasks over to a pro—then we'll cover how to work with an ad agency in Step 15. If neither of those options seem like a good fit, we'll discuss how to work with influencers in Step 16.

Study Both the Timeless and the Timely, but Avoid the Outdated

When it comes to learning about advertising, you want to focus on two areas. First, there are timeless lessons that can be learned from the advertising legends. These direct response pioneers learned the foundational aspects of advertising and wrote classic books. Learn from them. Second, you need to track the ultra-current information to answer the most important question, *what is working now?* Study the best advertising minds available to you. I've listed a set of blogs and podcasts to consider following below. What you want to avoid is being five years late to the party. There are trends in advertising tactics that work for a period of time, then decline. Stay current, and if you can afford to, work with an ad agency to make sure you're current. More on that in the next chapter.

The State of Instagram Advertising

Instagram advertising is booming. Each quarter it seems marketing budget is being shifted from Facebook advertising into Instagram advertising at healthy pace. At the time of this writing, the hottest ad option on Instagram is Story Ads. Whether that will continue or not isn't clear. But for now, it's certainly something to test. I'll show you how in the next few pages.

Advertising options on Instagram are changing fast. As with all the technical aspects of Instagram we've covered in this book so far, I'd encourage you to stay up to date with Instagram directly. It has fantastic tutorials, resources, success stories, and updates. You can see Instagram's advertising information at https://business.instagram.com/advertising/.

Prioritization and Advertising Rules for Success

Before we jump into the details, I think a word of advice is in order. First, I deliberately put this action step toward the end of the book for a very basic reason. You need to master the organic marketing tactics on Instagram before you focus on advertising. Prioritize the mastery of the organic marketing tactics first, then the advertising tactics second. If you do, you'll have both a strong organic marketing game and a strong advertising game. Put them together and you'll be unstoppable. But if you neglect the marketing fundamentals that we've covered thus far and start blowing money on advertising, your advertising won't perform as well as it otherwise could have. That is why it needs to be the second priority.

Over the years I've personally spent, or signed off on, over a million dollars in online advertising. Some of it was a wise investment, and some of it was a waste. So let me share a few things I've learned along the way. Hopefully these will give you some insights that you can apply to your situation. I call these my rules for success:

1. **Scatter lots of seeds—and water the ones that grow.** Most ads fail—and they fail for reasons you won't understand. It's frequently a mystery. So run lots of ads using a very small budget for each, maybe just $5. Then evaluate the result, and if it merits it, add more money. If not, kill it. The bigger your ad budget, the more small ads you have to set up and test.

2. **Remember—it's a money pit with no bottom.** You can waste a lot of money really fast using online advertising. Ads are literally a money pit with no bottom. In response, some people waste money on bad ads that should be shut off faster, while others refuse to spend enough money to test things properly. Both are mistakes. The remedy is to have a daily, weekly, and monthly budget and spend it as wisely as possible. At a minimum, if you're paying attention, you'll be learning things as you go.

3. **You probably suck at setting up ads.** I do. One time an "ad specialist" from Google called and offered me his help because he had seen I was spending a fair amount on Google AdWords. We got on a video call and he walked me through setting up an ad that he said would probably perform well. It did. A week later I was thrilled. But I could never replicate his results on my own. When I tried to set up the same type of ad, I lost lots of money and couldn't make it work. My conclusion was that I am an amateur at setting up ads and he's a professional. The 10,000-hour rule applies to advertising. Experience counts. Work with people who know what they're doing. If you don't, then you are the one investing in your own education—be a good student. But the investment of working with a pro will likely be well worth the cost.

4. **Don't burn money on dumb goals.** Do you know how much money has been spent by people trying to get followers on

Facebook, only to realize later that Facebook changed the game and followers don't even see their organically shared content? The value of that advertising diminished quickly over time. But learning how to put people onto your email list or make a sale, those are goals worth spending money on.

5. **Cars go faster if you keep pressing the gas pedal down.** Over time, it's easy to create a mental and emotional cap on your ad spending, kind of like a self-imposed speed limit. This happens even while your top line revenue grows. It's emotional, not logical. So, set an advertising budget rule, like 9 percent of your top line revenue will be spent on advertising. Stick to that percentage as you scale over the years.

6. **Think long-term—sometimes it's wise to lose money on ads.** If you can afford to acquire a customer at a loss because you know your long-term customer value (LTCV) is going to make it a winning idea over time, do it as much as you can afford. Don't guess at this stuff, that's gambling. Know your numbers. The bigger and better your back-end marketing, the more you can ramp up acquisition at a loss. If you don't know your LTCV, or have only one product, then don't play this game. But the more money you can make from people, and the faster you can make it, the more you can spend on acquiring customers. Keep one eye on your cash flow and the other on the longer-term horizon.

How to Set up Ads on Instagram

There are two primary methods for setting up paid ads on Instagram. First, you can do it directly underneath the content you've added, on the app itself. Simply tap the "Promote" button. If you've already promoted the content, the button will say "Promote Again" (Figure 14.1). This gives you a window into several campaign options that are intuitive and easy to follow. As long as you've already connected your Facebook business profile to your Instagram account, and you've got a credit card on file, then your ad setup will be quick and easy. If not, you'll need to complete those steps before you can move forward.

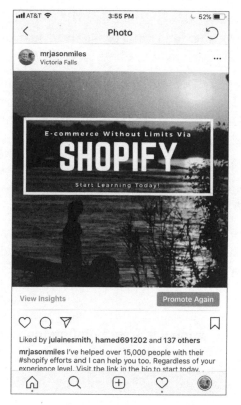

Figure 14.1 "Promote Again" Button

You can also set up and manage Instagram ads via the Facebook Ads Manager platform. Because of the advanced features and options, as well as the reporting functionality, this is the preferred method for more sophisticated advertisers.

The Types of Ads on Instagram

Let's dig into the Instagram advertising options. There are several types of ads on Instagram, and I'm sure more will be revealed in the future. The current options include:

- **Photo ads.** Photo ads are the simplest type of ad to run. Photo ads can either be square or landscape. They feature a call to action at the bottom of the image.

- **Video ads.** Video ads can be up to 60 seconds long. They can be shot in either landscape or square format. They autoplay with a call to action at the bottom of the video.

- **Carousel ads.** Instagram Carousel ads are a mixed media option. They can have between 2 and 10 images and/or video in any combination. Viewers swipe through the content. As with the other formats, the call to action is at the bottom.

- **Story ads.** Story ads appear on the Instagram Stories area. They include a full-screen, vertical format, and allow you to use both photos and video.

- **Slideshow ads.** The Slideshow ad feature plays like a video, but is made out of still photos. You can even add audio and text to your slideshow ad.

Audience Selection Options

Finding your ideal audience isn't hard. Using the Facebook Ads Manager you can target your ideal prospect by the following top-level topics—and each of these has a vast selection of subtopics:

1. **Location.** Target people by specific locations such as countries, states or provinces, or cities.

2. **Interests.** Reach people based on their interests. This is pulling from data such as apps they use, ads they click on, and accounts they follow.

3. **Behaviors.** Select people based on the activities they do both on and off Instagram and Facebook.

4. **Demographics.** Focus on a specific group by age, gender, or language.

5. **Custom audiences.** Focus on customers or prospects you already have identified via email or phone number.

Types of Calls to Action

There are several types of predefined calls to action on Instagram ads. Depending on the ad you choose, they might include:

1. **Visit profile.** This sends people to your profile, where ideally, they'll follow you, and the content of your bio and website link will compel them to learn more about you.

2. **Visit a business address.** For ads where learning the local address is most appropriate.

3. **Phone number.** For ads where a direct phone call is the most logical call to action.

4. **Learn more.** The call to action related to going deeper with educational content.

5. **Shop now.** The call to action related to purchasing a product.

6. **Watch more.** The call to action to see the longer form of a video.

7. **Contact us.** The call to action for direct conversations.

8. **Book now.** The call to action for calendaring- or scheduling-based marketing efforts.

9. **Sign up.** The call to action for class- or event-based marketing.

Viewing Results of an Ad

Instagram calls these your "Promotion Insights." You can view your Promotion Insights directly on the content piece you promoted by tapping the "View Results" link under the content (Figure 14.2). You'll see data related to:

1. **Interactions—Promotion Clicks.** The number of times the call to action was clicked on.

2. **Interactions—Profile Visits.** This will also show the percentage that comes from the promotion versus organic presentation.

3. **Interactions—Website Visits.** This also shows the percentage of organic versus paid results.

4. **Discovery—Reach.** How many people saw your content. The percentage of current profile followers vs. non-followers is shown.

5. **Discovery—New Followers.** The number of followers that came from the ad.

6. **Promotion—Spend.** The amount of your original budget you spent.

7. **Audience—Gender.** The percentage of women versus men.

8. **Audience—Age Range.** The ages of the audience you reached.

9. **Audience—Top Locations.** The top locations, by state, where you reached people.

Viewing Results of All Your Ads

If you'd like to see all the ads you've created—so you can evaluate how they've performed compared to each other, you can look in your Insights area. You access that via your Profile. Simply tap the links in the top right corner. Within the Insights area, click under the Content section, then scroll to the Promotions section and sort by the "See All" option.

Setting up Instagram Story Ads

Instagram Story Ads are created using the Facebook Ads Manager platform. They can be created with either a photo, a video, or a combination. The steps involved include:

1. Go to Facebook Ads Manager.

2. Click "Create Ad."

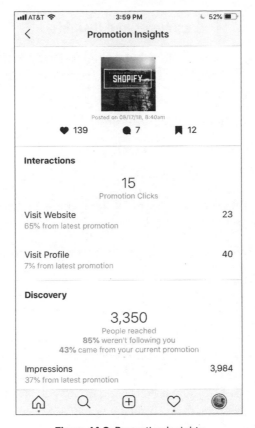

Figure 14.2 Promotion Insights

3. Select your marketing objective from either Brand Awareness, Reach, Traffic Objective, Lead Generation, App Installs, Conversions, or Video Views.

4. In the Placement Section select Automatic Placements or Edit Placements. Instagram Stories should be selected by default in either workstream.

5. Complete the steps to set up your ad campaign.

Resources and Insights

There are a huge number of Instagram advertising articles, tutorials, and walk-throughs online. Some of my favorite content can be found at the following websites:

1. https://business.instagram.com/advertising/

2. https://adespresso.com/blog/

3. https://blog.hootsuite.com

4. https://marketingland.com/library/channel/social-media
   -marketing

5. https://www.socialmediaexaminer.com/tag/instagram/

6. https://blog.bufferapp.com

7. https://sproutsocial.com/integrations/instagram/

In the next chapter, we'll discuss how to use an ad agency to take your Instagram advertising to the next level. Before you dismiss the idea as beyond your reach, don't. Innovative agencies are popping up that enable industrial-strength advertising at a fraction of the price you might expect. Keep reading, and let's figure out how to get your next step accomplished together!

SNAPSHOT

1. Instagram ads are easy to use and should be tested.

2. Use the Instagram app directly or the Facebook Ads Manager to create ads.

3. Test small and scale up if the return on investment justifies it.

Scale up Your Advertising with Agency Help

*Many a small thing has been made large
by the right kind of advertising.*

MARK TWAIN

If you've never done it before, working with an agency might feel a little intimidating. But the advantages are huge—and if you're going to take your Instagram marketing power to the next level, this will help! If you decide to take this step on your journey—the following benefits are yours to be had:

The 5 Benefits of Using an Agency

1. **Subject matter expertise.** Agencies start with talented and smart employees, then they make them perform at a high level every day, or clients get mad. That is a recipe for high-caliber outcomes. They learn every trick of the trade. Yes, it's tempting to toil away at advertising yourself since all the platforms are easy to learn and use, but be honest, do you really want to waste all that time learning what they already know?

2. **Cost savings.** There are three ways working with an agency helps you save money. First, you're not doing the work yourself, so you are freed up to make more money in better ways. Second, you don't have to hire staff—that may or may not be competent. But even if they are, payroll tax, benefits, and other hard costs can be avoided. Finally, and this is the biggest, your ads will be managed much more carefully from the start. Poor ad management is the single biggest money waster in this equation, and agencies are experts at riding herd on these runaway costs.

3. **Access to expert tools.** There are some tools, systems, and processes that you won't have access to, don't know about, and will never tap into on your own. Agencies are masters at finding and using industrial-strength marketing methods. Let them.

4. **Creative talent.** Most small-business owners aren't graphic artists. Yet, unless you're simply using Google Text Ads, then today's ad platforms require high-quality design. Ad agencies have professional in-house designers. But more than that—they know, after years of experience, what works on the platforms they advertise on. So they have both the graphic art chops and the feedback from thousands of ads.

5. **Discipline.** When I run my own advertising, I dabble. Turn it on, turn it off, get distracted, stop and go. That's no way to run a professional advertising effort. Working with an agency gives you the accountability you need to play the part of a professional that doesn't want to seem like a flake. So you do what you said you were going to do, stick with it, and treat the entire exercise with the respect it deserves.

Three Types of Instagram Agency Work

Currently there are three broad activities that Instagram agencies tend to do. Some do all three, some do two, and some do just one. Of course, you can do all of these things yourself without an agency, or you can keep one or two and let the agency do one. The combinations are almost endless. Getting clarity around what you're looking for—and what the agency offers—is the most important place to start. The three activities are:

1. **Account management.** As discussed in Step 8, having someone manage your daily FLCR (Follow-Like-Comment-Respond) work can be very helpful. Generally, a virtual assistant or specialized service provider offers these services in a stand-alone way. If an agency offers them as part of a comprehensive package, then you'll have to decide if that's the way you want to work.

2. **Advertising.** This work, which we'll cover more thoroughly for the rest of this chapter, includes managing the creative process for making ads, setting them up, monitoring the outcomes, split testing, managing the spending, and reporting back on results. Many of these companies have grown up doing Facebook advertising and are now focusing on Instagram as well. This is logical since the Facebook Ads Manager platform powers the ads on both social sites.

3. **Influencer marketing deals.** In the next chapter we'll dive into the world of influencer marketing more deeply. It has become a gold mine for marketers, and agencies have grown up around this exciting opportunity. A growing number of agencies do it as a specialty, but some will commingle it with account management and advertising management.

Evaluating an Advertising Agency

It can be hard to decide if an agency is right for you or not. There are multiple factors to evaluate. And while there are many agencies jumping into the world of Instagram advertising, not all of them have the depth of experience you might hope for. Here are a few tried-and-true criteria to consider.

1. Does the agency have undeniable client success stories and testimonials documenting outcomes from its Instagram-related work? Make sure its success stories include Instagram

specifically, not just Facebook or social media in general. We are looking for Instagram experts.

2. Does it have a clear and compelling mission and vision related to Instagram work? Many agencies are "jack of all trades, master of none" operators. So, while they'll be happy to run your Instagram efforts for you, they don't have a particular passion for Instagram and a body of knowledge built around the Instagram trade skills.

3. Do the agency's representatives express honest enthusiasm for working with you? Professional salespeople are in the business of telling you what you want to hear, so it's sometimes hard to discern sincerity, but there should be some spark of excitement for your product, service, or business. Look for signs that their minds are working creatively envisioning your near-term success.

4. Do they have a specific plan of action customized to your situation? Ask for a proposal that includes what they will do—and why. Have they listened to your unique situation? Did they pay attention when you were telling them about your competition, your industry, and your customer base? Have they factored in those elements?

5. Do you click with them on a personal level? Sometimes a good working relationship comes down to being able to communicate quickly and effectively with people because you share values, culture, communication style, temperament, and worldview. For example, if you have heartland of America values and they are "city slickers" from New York City (or vice versa), it is probably not going to be a good match. Work with people you are comfortable with, and life will be easier.

Ad Agency Pricing Models to Understand

The most important thing to consider when evaluating an agency is—can they help me grow revenue? The second thing to evaluate is how they do it. The third thing is whether they are credible and competent operators in that methodology. The final thing is the cost. But it's always top of mind for most frugal entrepreneurs, so let's get it out of the way up front. When starting with an agency it's important to understand how the agency makes money. There are a few common pricing models that you'll run into. Let's review them quickly.

1. **Flat fee pricing.** Many agencies charge a flat fee for a set number of services. This enables you to understand immediately whether you can afford them, and allows you to allocate a portion of your marketing budget to management costs. Depending on the service being delivered and the prestige of the agency, the fee could be almost any random number, from $299 a month to $25,000. There is no average, so do your best to explore all your options. In these situations the agency may require you to have a minimum ad spend on a monthly basis, or just have a recommendation. That amount would be on top of the flat fee.

2. **Percent of ad spend pricing.** Another common model is to simply charge you a percentage of your ad spend, say 15 percent. In this model, the agency will generally have a required minimum monthly spend—and may even lower its percentage when you spend more.

3. **Bespoke pricing.** Some agencies won't list their prices on their website, and instead have you request a "consultation" where they share the price after a vigorous sales pitch. They do that to avoid scaring away a good prospect with a high list price on their site, and because they know the close rate will be higher in that situation where they can answer questions and generally influence you with their charm and charisma.

4. **Campaign-specific pricing.** Some agencies will charge a flat one-time fee for a finite campaign, although most would rather turn you into a monthly recurring revenue stream. In some cases, supporting your one-time event, with a one-time marketing campaign fee is logical.

Enabling Agency Success

In fairness to any agency you begin working with, you need to extend the people you are working with a fair chance in a supportive way. Set them up for success in their efforts. To paraphrase legendary sports agent Jerry McGuire, you need to *help them help you*. Here is how to do it.

1. **Do what you say you're going to do.** No one likes to be strung along, lied to, or told one thing only to find out something else is going on. Be a person of integrity in your dealing with your agency, and if you say you're going to do something, work on something, have a certain timeline, or commit to a certain budget or process, then do it.

2. **Be a good communicator.** If there are problems, changes to the situation, or hard conversations to have, don't avoid them. Don't be passive-aggressive. Be honest and professional, and keep the lines of communication open.

3. **Give them your best.** There is nothing worse than working for a client that doesn't show up for appointments, reschedules constantly, doesn't pay attention when you are meeting, or doesn't spend the mental or emotional energy needed to co-create good outcomes.

4. **Be open-minded.** Only slightly worse than clients who don't give their best is one who already knows everything. This comes in two varieties. First, there is the "we already tried that—it won't work" closed-minded client. Second, there is the "I know more than any of you idiots about this topic—shut up and listen to me pontificate" client. If you want to demonstrate your super intelligence on the topic, then hire interns and boss them around. But treating an agency full of experts that way is a sign of an unhealthy ego.

5. **Set realistic expectations.** If you're not careful, when you initially set up a relationship with an agency, you can get gold fever. They are going to unlock 10X revenue growth, unlimited new customers, and worldwide fame. But this is an emotional setup for future letdown. Guard your expectations. The best

way to do that is treat it like an experiment. Don't expect success. Don't expect failure. Simply let their work be a test and come into it with an open mind.

Evaluating Agency Outcomes

When all is said and done, the only effective agency relationship that stands the test of time is one that delivers mutual value. A win/win for all involved. You get a good outcome—and the agency does too. How do you evaluate the results of your collaboration? Consider the following:

1. **Return on investment (ROI).** There is no getting around it. If your agency doesn't add incremental revenue, then it is not working well for you. Ideally, the ROI will be much more favorable than simply breaking even. How much more? That depends on a wide range of factors, including the industry you're in, your average order value, and lifetime customer value. When doing ROI work, you include the cost of the agency fee, plus the cost of the actual ads, and compare those together to the revenue generated.

2. **Return on ad spend, ROAS.** A much more narrow-focused metric, and a subset of the ROI, is the return on ad spend. This number looks exclusively at the result of the ad spending and compares it to the revenue generated.

The Challenges of Evaluating Success

In an ideal world, it would be easy to calculate ROI and ROAS. You'd simply get a report from your agency that says, "For every $1 you give us we are making you $5," and you'd say, "Great, here is a pile of money—let's scale it up! Billionaire time." Unfortunately, it rarely ever works so simply. Two of the most common technical challenges related to calculating returns are cross-device attribution and cross-platform attribution. Let's look at both briefly.

Cross-device attribution can be explained using the following example. Suzie sees your ad on her phone and likes it, clicks on it, and evaluates your offer, and then she goes to her computer, types in your URL, and completes the shopping experience. Does your ad get credit for that sale? No, since she changed devices.

Cross-platform attribution is similar. Here is an example. Suzie sees your ad on Instagram and engages with it, but doesn't complete a conversion goal (signup or sale). Then the following day, she sees your retargeting ad on Facebook and engages with it to complete the purchase. Did your Instagram ad campaign get any credit for the sale? Or should the retargeting campaign get all the credit?

The answers to these challenges are only found in thoughtful reflection on your data, and a big picture view of what is happening. Don't lose the forest for the trees. Your goal is to grow your revenue via advertising—and if that is happening, you're on the right track. Always be sure before you pronounce judgment on an ad agency, or a campaign, that you've looked at the factors holistically.

An Interview with the Team at Fetch & Funnel

Let's go behind the scenes and learn from Matt Lampkin and Samir ElKamouny, cofounders of Boston-based ad agency Fetch & Funnel, on Instagram @fetch.funnel (Figure 15.1). They specialize in Facebook and Instagram ads.

Q: How would you describe the Instagram services Fetch & Funnel offers?

A: We help e-commerce businesses scale faster through social advertising. We have our own proprietary methods, but like the dynamic nature of Facebook and Instagram, these methods are fluid and constantly updated to stay in tune as the landscape is continually evolving.

Facebook and Instagram are becoming more influential and relevant each day. As the fastest-growing social channel in the world, your customers live on Instagram. It's the place to be, and our services align with a data-driven approach designed to help businesses achieve the following:

Figure 15.1 Fetch & Funnel

- Increase the velocity of organic growth

- Leverage your audience voice amplification

- Prospect new customers through paid Instagram advertising

- Close the sale and track results through carefully curated retargeting campaigns

- Nurture your new customers and transition them into vocal brand advocates

Instagram is growing at a torrid pace—it's the future of social marketing. If your business is already running advertising campaigns and looking to double down and scale results, we can help make this happen.

Q: Who are your ideal clients?

A: Our ideal clients are forward thinking e-commerce brands that take Facebook and Instagram seriously. You have already tested the waters and invested marketing budgets into social advertising. You understand the value, see the potential, but haven't yet been able to achieve or scale your successes.

Q: Broadly speaking, what do you think the opportunities on Instagram include for small businesses?

A: Small businesses have a massive opportunity to not only reach their ideal customers, but to reach targeted, hyper-local audiences through paid advertising as well. I'm amazed at what small businesses are able to achieve on Instagram. There are millions of hyper-local influencers with niche audiences comprised of your ideal customers! I guarantee it, all you need to do is find them.

The ability to showcase products, services, culture, beliefs, you name it. The key is to translate the story behind why your business exists, and give it some personality. Whether it be lifestyle shots, your product or service (or staff) in action, I encourage everyone to tell their own unique story. It's real, it's life. This is what people love.

Q: Are there entrepreneurs or small-business owners that aren't a good fit?

A: It's hard for me to think of a business that wouldn't benefit from it. However, a gas station or a small taxi service may need to work a bit harder. But think about this, what if you post funny memes around gas attendees or gas-related jokes. Grow your followers, always tag your location, and then put together a special offer and tell your audience. They'll show up! Imagine scrolling through your feed and an account says fill up tonight, prices increase tomorrow. I know I'm headed to go and fill up my car on the way home tonight . . .

Q: For entrepreneurs or small-business owners trying to decide between using an agency or having an intern or a lower-priced assistant manage their account—what would you say?

A: Honestly, it's super dependent on the business, but I would say in almost all instances both would be best. An intern can help with the actual management of the account. As long as they have a basic knowledge of Instagram, they can take and post product shots, repost customer photos, and create a theme. Then you use an agency like us to bring your account to the next level. We achieve this through consulting, assisting with boosting engagement and followers, and assisting with overall strategy. The two create a powerful yet relatively inexpensive punch.

Q: As an agency, using Instagram to attract clients, what is your Instagram content and/or advertising strategy?

A: For us it's all branding. Know the brand that you're trying to communicate. Then post photos and content that build and reinforce what you want to stand for. Know your ideal audience, and then do the research to find out where they spend their time on Instagram. Which accounts do they follow? What are their interests, their demographics, their locations. When do they like to absorb content, what types of content do they prefer?

We've gone through a lot of testing, we've experimented on ourselves and learned a lot. We've even built out a few playful accounts for additional experimentation. Right now most of our content is a combination of blog articles demonstrating thought leadership along with great lifestyle photos from our team. Fetch & Funnel is a 100 percent remote company, our employees frequently work internationally for extended periods of time. We aim to reach new customers through dissemination of knowledge, along with future marketing rock stars that want to join a team that believes work should be adapted to fit into our lives, not the other way around.

Q: Anything else you'd like to share with readers that I haven't asked about?

A: Try to work with influencers and see if you're able to achieve positive results. If you haven't already tapped into the power of influencers, you're likely missing out. Find accounts with followers that align with your target market, reach out to the account owner, and simply ask if they might be willing to promote your product or service. You can get into risk analysis, but really just try to get several that are inexpensive and try it out! It's often one of the lowest cost-per-impression tactics you can find. If they have the influence, you might be able to see higher conversion rates than any ads you'll run. Cheap impressions plus higher conversion rates equals great ROI.

Q: If readers are interested in learning more about your services, how can they get connected?

A: We'd be happy to personally connect and give readers a free consultation session if they think working with an agency is a good next step for them. Send an email to contact@fetchfunnel .com or visit our website at FetchFunnel.com, click the Facebook chat icon in the bottom right, and we'll have a live conversation.

SNAPSHOT

1. Consider using agency help.

2. Be sure you're a good client.

3. Understand the pricing models that agencies use.

Start Working with Influencers

*There are exceptional people out there who are capable
of starting epidemics. All you have to do is find them.*

MALCOLM GLADWELL

Social media influencers are eager to monetize their hard work by advertising on your behalf, and the biggest social media influencer platform has quickly become Instagram. Influencer marketing has become a whole industry that is making powerful waves in the world of online marketing.

In this chapter, we'll dive into this exciting new world and walk you through how to set up an influencer marketing effort in a professional and ongoing way. Then we'll sit down with an influencer marketing insider, Dan Fernandez, and get his insider tips.

Influencer Marketing Defined

According to the leading marketing blog in this exciting new marketing space, Influencer Marketing Hub, www.influencermarketinghub .com, influencer marketing is "the process of identifying individuals who create high-impact conversations, with your ideal target audience; building relationships, by engaging and supporting these influencers to promote a brand's product or services." The core platforms influencer marketing seems to operate best on are Instagram and YouTube, although some influencers have a large reach onto other platforms, too, such as Twitter, Snapchat, Twitch, and Facebook, and of course, their own blog or email list.

The Difference Between Mass Media Influencers and Social Influencers

What's the difference between the old paradigm, aka celebrity endorsements helping you on mass media projects, and this new way of working with social media influencers? The old way was fairly well established—find a person of influence and cut a deal with him or her to talk about your product in your TV, radio, or print advertising. If you had a big marketing budget, you could afford to work with an A-list celebrity and run primetime TV commercials or print ads in premiere publications. If you had a smaller budget, no worries, you could still find a TV actor from a 1990s era show and run your commercials at 2:00 a.m. This was not a game for the local retailer, solopreneur, self-published author, or similar small budget marketer. It just didn't make sense.

The new influencer paradigm is much simpler. You work with influencers who have their own audience. They generally do the creative for you, and publish it to their audience. You can still use only one national influencer if you want, or you can work with dozens, hundreds, or thousands of influencers who have a smaller, but still meaningful, reach. This unlocks massive untapped potential and opens the doors for marketers with smaller budgets.

Three Reasons Marketers Like Influencers

What marketers have found is a nice collection of benefits associated with this form of marketing. First, this method of marketing feels less financially risky than big expensive campaigns that feature just one celebrity. It's more like placing a small wager on a huge number of bets. Some will pay off. Second, it also lowers the risk of celebrity-induced scandal. Having one celebrity endorser—who gets arrested or caught up in some huge scandal—tends to ruin your marketing. Finally, and this is the most exciting part for us little guys, it lowers the barrier to entry, so smaller businesses with smaller marketing budgets can get in on this game. For all these reasons, influencer marketing is super hot.

Five Tiers of Influence

All of this is still relatively new and therefore somewhat undefined. Different agencies and bloggers define influencer impact differently, but it seems the industry is sorting influencers into five common levels that marketers are beginning to specifically focus on in different ways. You'll have to decide how to organize your influencer marketing work. Many marketers, bloggers, and industry insiders are using a framework like this:

- **Nano influencers**—From 10 to 1,000 followers.

- **Micro influencers**—From 1,000 to 10,000 followers

- **Macro influencers**—From 10,000 to 100,000 followers

- **Mega influencers**—From 100,000 to 1,000,000 followers

- **Celebrity influencer**—More than 1,000,000 followers

Which level is right for you? Marketing analytic specialists are already starting to do formal studies to determine which type of influencer is best to work with from an ROI perspective, but I would caution you not to make assumptions based on general articles. Do your own analysis. One fun tool to do research with is the Influencer Marketing Hub Micro-influencers vs. Celebrities calculator. You can use it to do a head-to-head comparison of any two Instagram accounts. Check it out at https://influencermarketinghub.com/micro-influencers-vs -celebrities/#. So who is a better influencer to work with, Anna Saccone or Jonathan Joly? Let's see (Figure 16.1).

Ultimately there will likely be a good use case for working with every type of influencer. Who you work with as a marketer will come down to a set of campaign variables such as budget, product type, niche or industry, etc. At a minimum, you should start to test working with each type of influencer and see the impact on your business. Maybe for you casting a wide net with nano and micro influencers will perform better than working with one mega influencer. You won't know until you test it. Don't depend on generalizations from bloggers or data analysts. Test your way to success.

How Much to Pay for Influencer Marketing

The range of pay for influencer work can range from literally zero to millions. But as the market matures, the ranges are becoming standardized. Let's look at each.

Commonly nano and micro influencers are happy to work for freebies, VIP treatment, or reciprocal marketing of some type. In other words, noncash incentives. This looks different in different industries, but commonly it's free meals from restaurants or free lodging from travel brands. It's free clothing and accessories from fashion brands. You get the idea. The list is endless. These influencers are working to build their credibility, their ad-based income systems, and their list of clients. As Les Brown would say, "They're Huuuungry."

There is a point where micro influencers begin to recognize their value based on the level of inquiries they begin to receive and they transition from perks to cash. It's different for each influencer because of their unique situation and audience. Tapinfluence, a leading influencer platform, states the average influencer on its platform makes $763.50 a month. That number seemed sort of low to me, but when I mentioned it to my wife, she said, "Wow, that's really cool."

Influencers with less than 10,000 followers get $75 a post on Independent UK, a platform representing influencers. Captive8, an influencer agency, says Instagram influencers with 100,000 followers can command $5,000 a post. Influencers with a reach of 500,000 to a million can charge between $5,000 and $10,000 per post, according to HYPR, another marketplace in the space. When you do the math, you begin to see that on Instagram a common metric is between $5 and $10 per 1,000 followers. Of course, these prices are changing as the market grows.

But followers isn't everything. Post engagement is a more meaningful metric, since it directly relates to the actual influence the

Figure 16.1 Jonathan Joly vs. Anna Saccone

influencer has on his or her tribe. According to Tony Tran, CEO of the influencer marketing platform Lumanu, you can expect to pay from 25 to 75 cents per post engagement. So, $250 to $750 for every 1,000 post engagements. These prices will change over time. And prices also depend on whether you are working with an influencer direct, or working via a platform.

The point is, this is quickly becoming a healthy and long-term advertising channel. It's turning into a true two-sided market where supply (influencers who are willing to monetize their tribe via advertising work) and demand (marketers willing to pay for that work) is quickly becoming refined.

How to Find Influencers

There are several methods for finding the right influencers to connect with. Let's review the most popular. I think you'll find using a platform or service is the wisest way to go.

Search Instagram. Of course, you can scour Instagram to find the right type of influencers in your niche or industry and collect their information for future follow-up. Two common ways would be to look at who influential people are following, or which posts get the most engagement in connection to hashtags you care about. Obviously, this is less than ideal, since many influencers operate on multiple channels including their blog, Facebook, Instagram, YouTube, Pinterest, and beyond. The second challenge quickly becomes—how do you keep track of the details with all the influencers? This gives rise to the need for a matchmaking tool.

Hire a researcher. A second option is to hire a researcher to do the research work for you. This works well for solving the challenge of identifying influencers, but not for organizing contacts or campaigns. These researchers get you the information you're looking for, without you having to do all the heavy lifting yourself. They give you a list of influencers, based on your criteria, and then you reach out to set up the deals. To hire a researcher, visit the sites we've previously mentioned in the book, including Fiverr.com and Upwork.com.

Use a marketplace. A growing number of influencer agencies have created proprietary platforms where influencers register, explain who they are, and prepare for your exciting contact. Then marketers can join to find influencers, organize details, and manage the process. Think of eharmony, but for influencers and marketers. The catch? The agencies don't generally give the marketers access for free. They sell it to you. Time will tell which of the marketplaces win over time, but here is a partial list to start with:

- Tomoson: www.tomoson.com

- TapInfluence (part of Izea): https://www.tapinfluence.com

- AspireIQ (formerly Revfluence): www.aspireiq.com

- NeoReach: www.neoreach.com

- Mavrck: www.mavrck.co

- Upfluence: www.upfluence.com

- Izea: www.izea.com

- HYPR Brands: www.hyprbrands.com

- Julius Works: www.juliusworks.com

- True North Social: www.truenorthsocial.com

- Viral Nation: www.viralnation.com

- Lumanu: www.lumanu.com

- Popular Chips: www.popularchips.com

- Traackr: www.traackr.com

What Can Influencers Do for You?

The list of what influencers can do for you is pretty long. The sky is really the limit in terms of your ability to engage with them creatively. Here are a few of the more common activities:

1. **Discount codes or coupons.** Give the influencer a discount code to share in a post. This is a great option because you can give each influencer a unique code and immediately see which one has an audience that works best for your offer.

2. **Affiliate code.** Similar to coupon codes, but for long-term marketing, set them up as an affiliate with a unique tracking code. The question in this arrangement is whether they get a percentage of sales earned, like many affiliate marketing programs offer, or if you simply use the code as a mechanism to track their sales.

3. **Influencer takeover.** Have the influencers manage your account for a day. This can be fun since they announce it to their tribe and in theory, those people come see what is happening on your profile and hopefully like it and begin following you.

4. **Guest post on your profile.** Have them post content on your profile. Then they can share it with their tribe and it serves as an enticement for their tribe to come visit your profile.

5. **A social media mention.** Have them simply mention your Instagram profile in a post.

6. **Sponsored post.** Have them make a post and tag you in it. Ideally this is done with a nice product photo or video where they are interacting with your product.

7. **Long-term ambassador role.** Work with them as a brand ambassador for a set period of time. If you do, then you'll want to define what activities they engage in on your behalf.

8. **Giveaway.** Have them host a giveaway of your product.

Avoiding Fraudulent Influencers

It is so easy to buy fake followers these days that smart marketers need to be sure they don't get ripped off by prospective influencers. There are a couple of ways to do this wisely. First, use marketplaces to find your influencers. They will generally have safeguards that ensure your prospective influencer has real followers. Second, you can also use a free audit tool that analyzes Instagram accounts and gives you a health report. I like the one from Influencer Marketing Hub, found here: https://influencermarketinghub.com/instagram-fake-follower -bot-checker-free/. You can find a similar version of the tool on Hype Auditor, www.hypeauditor.com. Finally, you should always test small. Do the minimum viable test with any new influencers. After they've proven they have an audience that is responsive to your offer, use them again and up the creative effort.

25 Example Calls to Action to Give to Your Influencers

Not sure what call to action to ask influencers to use? John Koch (remember him from Step 7?) recommends three examples that you can customize—I've included them below. To find even more ideas, I turned to an invaluable little book I've used over the years and adapted some of the phrases. The book is *Words That Work* by Richard Bayan. You should pick up a copy. Use these ideas to get started:

- [ ] Follow @username for amazing (insert your niche) posts!
- [ ] Follow @username to get (insert benefit here)!
- [ ] Follow @username for hot deals!
- [ ] I'm loving the @username posts—follow them!
- [ ] I think you'll really like @username—follow them!
- [ ] Follow @username and put your business on top of the competition.
- [ ] Gain an unfair advantage by following @username!
- [ ] Want an edge? Follow @username!
- [ ] It's easier than ever to (insert desired action of niche prospects) follow @username
- [ ] @username wants to be your go-to expert. Follow him/her!
- [ ] Learn what works and what doesn't—follow @username!
- [ ] Learn how others are succeeding—follow @username!
- [ ] Follow @username, the market leader in (insert niche)
- [ ] Get high performance tools and tips—follow @username!
- [ ] Get huge deals @username
- [ ] Get authentic insights—follow @username
- [ ] Attract (insert desired niche attribute)—follow @username
- [ ] Take the first step toward (desired niche attribute) follow @username
- [ ] Turn your free time into learning time, follow @username
- [ ] Fine-tune your (insert desired skill) follow @username
- [ ] @username will change your life!
- [ ] Learn new competitive skills—follow @username
- [ ] Get personal coaching @username
- [ ] Get the training you need from @username
- [ ] Let go of (insert least desired emotion or challenge) follow @username

GET 75 MORE INFLUENCER CALLS TO ACTION

I've included another 75 prewritten calls to action in the Instagram Power Expansion Pack—be sure to get a copy at www.winning.online.

An Interview with Tomoson Founder Dan Fernandez

Tomoson (@tomosonreviews on Instagram) is an influencer marketplace with 90,000 influencers. Check it out at www.tomoson .com. Tomoson offers several unique features compared to other marketplaces, and we'd encourage you to check them out. I went one-on-one with the founder, Dan Fernandez, and I think you'll really enjoy this interview!

Q: How does Tomoson assist influencers and marketers to leverage the opportunities for online influence?

A: We're really focused on getting brands to be able to connect with an influencer and see what the influencer actually has for statistics as well as filter and search by those statistics so that they can start to find people that, depending on their marketing goals, can be drastically different. We have brands that are, for example, looking for a lot of micro influencers, so they may not really care for the people with 100,000 pieces of engagement.

The other thing that we do on the influencer side is we allow influencers to have a marketplace for campaigns where they can filter, search, apply for, and actually interact with these brands so that it's one centralized location based on what kind of categories.

Q: The shift toward influencer marketing—why do you think it's happening, and where do you see it going in the next year or two?

A: in the next two years I think they've said it's going to increase 25 to 50 percent from where it's at right now. The reason for the success of it is pretty obvious, just based on the success of social media, but it's just another medium for building an ad. You don't see as many ads on magazines and you don't interact with them, whereas those ads that are on social media you can either interact with, or you can relate to the person, so it can be seen on a more personal and real level.

It can be somebody that is actually using the product in real life, you can get better perspective on it, you can get an opinion on the little intricacies, like when you do an unboxing for a new Samsung phone or whatever. Brands love it because that marketing has, depending on the influencer you work with, infinite shelf life. It can be continuously shared, which just gives the brand a much better ROI in the long haul. From both sides, it gives the influencer content and ability to make money and it gives the brand the ability to have an advertisement that can be making money for them for a long, long time.

Q: Tomoson is unique compared to a lot of the other influencer marketplaces because you list the freebies and also the deals so that they are publicly visible on your site, which is fun for influencers and marketers, I would imagine. Talk to me more about that. Is that important in our business model, and how did you guys come to set that part of it up?

A: We had a lot of Amazon brands that wanted to leverage us. They wanted some features beyond just straight influencer marketing. The ability to have the deals was based around that. We wanted to display everything because when we started we just wanted to put it all out there. We wanted to be as transparent as possible because we felt that a lot of the other platforms were hiding things. It just never made sense to us. Allowing a brand to see everybody that's willing to apply to a campaign and having that open marketplace, a lot of times helped the brands, because more often than not the brands didn't even know what they wanted.

We would say, "What are you looking for in an influencer?" They would go, "Yeah, give me somebody that's only a pet blogger." We'd go, "Okay. What happens if a fashion influencer applies and they're taking pictures with their dog but they're really a fashion influencer and they have great influence? You don't want to work with them?" They'd say, "Yeah, include them too." So allowing a wider range of influencers to apply and then allowing the brand to filter the people on their dashboard that have applied so that it's an easier connection. The only way that we really found to do this was to just open it up because at the time when we started we didn't have the sophisticated algorithms that are out now.

Q: From a marketer's perspective, what's the process for adding a campaign to Tomoson? I notice there's paid opportunities, freebies, and discount deals?

A: You register, it's a free 21-day trial. You can go in, you can create your campaign. When you create the campaign, it asks you what your initial marketing goal is: are you looking to give a product away for free, are you looking to work with a big influencer, are you looking to do social deals. Then you set your budget. Budget is just a way to help us determine what kind of influencers we should potentially recommend to you. You could put whatever you want for your budget, you could put $0 if you want. Then you add your product details.

Or, it could be digital content. That's the new one, the content distribution campaign, where you don't need to physically send a product to an influencer, you could simply say, "Hey, retweet my post, reshare this video, put this PDF out there." Brands are really loving it because they may have some really great sales material or funny content or whatever. Then they're getting other influencers to retweet it, reshare it, repost it on Instagram, like it, comment it, tag it. That's really helping jump-start some of the brand's social media content because at the end of the day it takes the influencers two seconds to click a button. I've seen an influencer get paid $2,000 just for clicking share, and it helped the brand explode this post.

Then our team reviews it on the back end to make sure all the links are accurate and everything is correct, and then it gets published live in our marketplace. Then influencers will just start applying, and you can either invite additional influencers or just let it go and see who comes into your campaign.

Q: So, in a way your service works like 99designs, where people with the talent basically apply to your campaign, raise their hand in essence. Is that right?

A: That is correct. You filter, you vet it, you can build your short list, and then you say, "These are the people I want to hire." You can check the box, click hire, hire them all at once. If you're paying them, the nice thing is we have an escrow system so you can deposit funds into escrow, it sits there, and then that way you know as a brand that until the influencer actually does what they say, funds will not be released and you can verify it. That's the system that everybody's got, but it really helps on both sides of the coin because as a brand you know they're good for it and vice versa, the influencer knows you're actually going to get paid. It essentially builds a contract between the two of them.

Q: What does an average campaign budget look like, what's the average price range?

A: It's hard to say an average. I would say if you come in with $500 a month that's plenty to start. Think of it like Google AdWords, how much would you start with Google AdWords? They say you need to figure out your data, you probably need to spend at least in my opinion 500 bucks to even figure out which AdWords are working, what's working correctly, what's driving traffic, what's getting likes, et cetera. You can do the freebie offers and there's plenty of ways to do that, but I typically like to say start with $500.

One of the best tricks, and it takes more work, but if you have either a VA or you're willing to put the time and effort in, once you pick our influencers, look through their existing content and see which post got the most engagement. There will be one or two that will jump out. Look at that image, look at the messaging and figure out a way to work with that influencer to almost repurpose that same look, message, whatever, with your brand or product. You know that whatever was said right there or done right there resonates with their audience.

Q: A lot of people cite your guys' research on ROI. I've seen you quoted a lot with the basic commentary that for every $1 spent on influencer marketing marketers are getting $6.50 back in return on investment. Can you just walk us through that a little bit, when was that survey done, how solid was the research? It's getting played around the Internet a lot. It's a big statement.

A: I know. Honestly, that's a good four years old now. When we did it we pulled our database of brands and we sent out email surveys to them. I think we had 10,000 emails we sent out. We got back I want to say close to 200 responses. That's the number we came up with. I would definitely say it's lower now. You've got to spend more with influencers now than you did four years ago.

Influencers are realizing that they're worth money, so they're charging more. I've seen them having a shelf life on their posts now. Some influencers say, "Hey, I only leave my posts up for one month if they're paid unless you're willing to pay the additional 200 bucks to keep it up forever. They're getting wise to this stuff. You could still make money, but if we were to run it again I would guarantee it would probably be half of that.

Q: Let me ask you about micro influencers versus major influencers in terms of who you work with. Does Tomoson mostly have micro, or do they have everybody? What do you say for a new marketer coming into it, how should they look at the differences between the two?

A: I would say the majority of ours, if we did 80/20, the 80 percent is micro to small influencers where the mega, huge, celebrities, are 20 percent of our demographic.

The difference I see between the micro and the big-time influencers is two things. Micro influencers, you've got to use a lot of them to really get the same impact. I'm also going to be spending $500, $1,000, $2,000 for a major influencer, compared to the micro influencer, where I'm just probably giving away a product. Micro influencers can be pretty powerful just because of their level of engagement.

The flip side, the actual professional influencer, the big influencers, yeah, that's where then you really need to look at your ROI. "Hey, I just spent $2,000 with this person. What was my goal? Was my goal just to get a bunch of likes to my page? Drive traffic?

The other forgotten asset of influencer marketing is the actual digital content itself. You could go work with an influencer just to produce a video because they're willing to do it for 500 bucks, but if you went to a videographer they would charge $5,000. They post it on their YouTube page and then they send you the video, a double win.

Q: For marketers looking to begin using influencers, do you have two or three top tips?

A: Yes. Do your research when you're first starting. Think outside that box. Next, understand your product, your market, and what you're looking to accomplish because that'll give you a goal. Then, the biggest thing I can say is one-and-done marketing never works. If you only have $2,000 to do on influencer marketing, spread that out over four months. You're going to make mistakes on probably those first couple to figure out what you're doing.

Then the last thing, if you're working with influencers, it's your first time and you're trying to get the attention of a big-time influencer, money talks and keep your message short and sweet. Hit them up on all their channels because I guarantee they have a lot of channels that are just there and one is their primary. Hit them on all of them, hit them multiple times. These big guys are contacted so often, so hit them up as often as you can if you find somebody that you really want to work with.

SNAPSHOT

1. Influencer marketing is here to stay.

2. Use marketplaces to find influencers.

3. Decide what they can do for you and begin testing campaigns.

4. Consider Tomoson a resource for finding micro influencers.

Become an Influencer

A referral influences people more than the best broadcast message. A trusted referral is the holy grail of advertising.

MARK ZUCKERBERG

Maybe it's time to consider becoming an influencer yourself? In this chapter, we'll discuss practical tips you can use to monetize your tribe. We'll share tools and resources to help you understand the opportunity. Plus, we'll go one-on-one with influencer Alejandro Reyes to learn how he built a thriving six-figure influencer business working with companies like Disney, Chase, and Target.

How Much Is Your Current Account Worth?

Let's start with the basic question. If you logged into one of the influencer marketplaces, how much could you start making right now? Check out the handy tool at: https://influencermarketinghub.com /instagram-money-calculator/ to see an estimate of how much you could currently make given your current Instagram account size.

How Much Time Will It Take?

As you might guess, everyone is different with different goals and diligence, but the key takeaway from the articles and comments is—this is a full-time job if you plan to take it seriously. According to their 2017 Influencer Marketing State of the Union Report, Influencer Marketplace Hashoff reports the following breakdown of daily work hours:

- 10% spend more than 10 hours.

- 7% spend 8–10 hours.

- 11% spend 7–8 hours.

- 34% of influencers spend 4–7 hours.

- 28% spend 2–4 hours.

- 10% spend 1–2 hours.

- 1% spend less than an hour.

14 Top Tips from Successful Influencers

The founder of *Authority* magazine, Yitzi Weiner, recently asked influencers to share their experiences and top tips. He compiled the interviews in a massive post on Medium titled "75 Prominent Influencers Share Their Top Advice on How to Become an Influencer" that has roughly 375 tips. I'd encourage you to check it out at: https://medium.com/thrive-global/75-prominent-influencers-share-their-top-advice-on-how-to-become-an-influencer-1ebbe31abbb4. Here are 14 of the most notable tips and links to the influencers who shared them.

- **Top Tip 1: Platform selection.** I found a new platform that was fun to create content on. Trying to build an audience on an established platform is much harder than an up and coming platform. I picked Musical.ly and live.ly. —From Austin Iuliano, @austiniuliano.

- **Top Tip 2: Inbound content.** To be an influencer, you must publish high-quality unique content. It's best to create content via multiple channels like video, blog, podcast, and social media. —From Kean Graham, CEO of MonetizeMore.com.

- **Top Tip 3: Don't strive to be an influencer.** Becoming an influencer isn't a goal unto itself; it's what happens when others react to your work and message in a way that moves them. The clearer your message, the more genuine it is, and the more persistent and consistent you are with relaying that message, the more people you are likely to influence and the more lives you are likely to change. —Kelly Hayes-Raitt, author and founder of House Sit Diva, https://housesitdiva.com.

- **Top Tip 4: Do more than one thing.** Take advantage of all avenues of content marketing, including blogging, vlogging, podcasting, and ebooks. —Kimberly Gauthier, Dog Nutrition Blogger and Author, Keep the Tail Wagging®.

- **Top Tip 5: Leverage events using hashtags.** A really fun way to increase followers is to be active during big events like the Oscars or the Super Bowl. By posting witty, funny, or shocking things during these events (using the unique hashtags) you can end up on the trending page, and ultimately drive more views to your page and increase your following. —Torri Webster is a Toronto based-media personality and actor with 297,000 Instagram followers, @torriwebster.

- **Top Tip 6: Deliver actionable advice.** As an influencer, people are not only looking to be inspired by your image and motivational speeches, they want to learn from you the right ways and exact steps to achieve certain results. They might be attracted to you because of your brand, but they are only going to stay and come back because of the value they get out of it, so you have to be constantly delivering actionable advice that they can apply to their lives. —Rania Hoteit, CEO and Founder of ID4A Technologies. On Instagram @raniahoteit_officialpublicpage.

- **Top Tip 7: Set a budget for promotion.** I currently promote at least 40 percent of my content. Much of my income as an influencer goes into promotion. With new Instagrammers jumping onboard every single day, you want to make sure that you are discoverable. In addition, change where you promote your content. I fluctuate between Westchester County, New York City, and even the Miami area during the winter because I know Hamptonites vacation/live in and around there during the colder months. —Vanessa Gordon, Publisher, East End Taste Magazine. On Instagram @eastendtaste.

- **Top Tip 8: Quality.** Be consistent with your aesthetic. Keep your content high quality. Do you know how to operate a camera? Shoot videos? Do you know how to edit and select the *best* photo from the 100 you just took? Learning to discern what images and videos will rack up the most engagement is crucial. —Mae Karwowski, Founder and CEO, Obvious.ly. On Instagram @obviously.

- **Top Tip 9: Walk it like you talk it.** If you are imploring others to do something, do it too. Whether it's meditation, exercise, or anything else you want others to practice, the authenticity of your ask is felt by others. You want to be a product of your own work and you literally are a walking representation of your brand. —Cheryl Sutherland, Founder of PleaseNotes. On Instagram @please_notes.

- **Top Tip 10: Be expert.** The first tip to becoming an influencer is becoming an expert in your field—know your subject and be able to contribute thoughtfully to the genre that you're passionate about. —Jessica Wright, Founder of the travel blog, Bon Traveler. On Instagram @bontraveler.

- **Top Tip 11: It truly is a labor of love, patience is the key in this game**. You have to be willing to take losses before the wins come. —Ronaldo Linares On Instagram @chef_ronaldo_ and @vibranthealth.

- **Top Tip 12: Provide edutainment.** Value plus entertainment is the magical combination in a busy world with seemingly infinite competition for people's eyeballs. —Amy Burton Matriarch of LuckyFortune8Family on YouTube (with over 48 million views and 100,000 subscribers on YouTube alone). On Instagram @luckyfortune8family.

- **Top Tip 13: Know what you want.** Having direction and clarity of mind will help you move forward with confidence. The great Stephen Covey, mega best-selling author of *The 7 Habits of Highly Effective People* and someone who endorsed my book, perhaps said it best: If the ladder is not leaning against the right wall, every step we take just gets us to the wrong place faster. —Jonathan Alpert, Manhattan and Washington, D.C., psychotherapist, Wall Street performance coach, and author of *Be Fearless: Change Your Life in 28 Days.* On Instagram @jonathanalpert.

- **Top Tips 14: Only promote what you believe in.** Social media can be such a crowded, oversaturated place and it can feel like some influencers are shoving fake inspiration down your throat. If you're promoting something, be it a cause or an idea, make sure your following knows why you're doing it. —Heidi Wong is a social media influencer with over 130,000 followers. On Instagram @heidiwongofficial.

WHICH PLATFORMS TO SIGN UP FOR?

Influencer platforms are battling for dominance currently, so there are lots of options. Refer to the list in Step 16 and evaluate their pros and cons.

An Interview with Influencer Alejandro Reyes

In a prior chapter I mentioned a work colleague, Alejandro Reyes, @alejandroreyes on Instagram. In the last few years he's built an exciting six-figure influencer business using multiple channels, with the anchor being YouTube. On YouTube, ThatReyesFamily (Figure 17.1).

Figure 17.1 Alejandro Reyes

I asked him to give us the insider details, and he shared some fantastic tips. Here's that conversation:

Q: Can you tell us about your experience in influencer marketing, when did you start, what was the goal?

A: We started in 2014 with a YouTube channel, and as a result of growing an audience it's pushed us to Facebook and Instagram. The goal initially was to really influence people and impact people in a positive way. It had nothing to do with money, it had to do with two things, (1) we wanted to record our girls so we could make memories, and (2) we wanted to inspire people to have a happy life.

Q: How has it gone—are there successes you've achieved that you've been excited about?

A: We've been blown away by the results, we focused on a niche. The niche for us was family vlogging, but then it was like—how do you differentiate yourself from the thousands of other people that are coming to be influencer marketers—for us it was the niche within the niche was a Hispanic family. So we have been successful with that small segment because there aren't a lot of other influencers in that sub-niche. It's really easy to get discouraged when you see other influencers with millions of followers, but there is very little competition when you niche down. We've had a lot of success out of it. With a fairly small reach we've been able to create several years of six-figure income from brand deals. We've done deals with companies like Disney, Chase, Target, and Dove, just to name a few.

Q: Do you feel like the opportunity to be an influencer is over, or is there still room for a lot more people?

A: There is massive room, but it's more competitive, and because of that I think you need to be more strategic. You need to have a recipe—seeing what other people are doing in other niches and figuring out how that can work for you. It's the only way to succeed because there is more competition. The best strategy wins.

Q: What would you share as tips or suggestions for people hoping to become an influencer?

A: The first one is, again, niche selection. It's like picking a niche that is underserved that you can also be passionate about— because passion is what leads to the next point, which is consistency. If you're not pumped about a topic you're probably not going to post pictures and videos. But if you're pumped about it—it's going to feel more like a hobby than work. It's more of a passion—you'll post consistently.

Q: Are there tools, platforms, or third-party apps you use to help run your work?

A: For YouTube, we use VidIQ, it's a great way to find out what people are searching for. Then for relationship management, we use a Google Sheet of all the deals we've done, who the contacts are, the offers, etc. Having it in one place lets you see the differences between a YouTube deal, an Instagram deal, a Facebook deal.

Q: What do you see as the differences between influencer work on YouTube vs. Instagram?

A: I think it has everything to do with engagement on all the channels. On YouTube, it's more personality driven. On Instagram, it's more topical. I have friends who have very large Instagram accounts that post recipes, and the brands they work with are just looking at engagement. Like, yes, you have a million people following you, but you literally got 37 likes on your last post? So engagement is critical on all the platforms. For example, I just heard about Liza Cotje, she is a YouTuber with 10 million subscribers. She recently did a deal with Beats by Dre, and I think I saw that she sent five times as many clicks as any other celebrity they had previously used combined.

Q: What do you see as the future of influencer marketing— where is it headed?

I think brands are moving away from traditional deals and looking to influencers who have engagement. So, I think we're just barely scratching the surface when it comes to people creating content that will work well for big brands. I think family friendly is important. As an example, you have people who have large audiences who curse a lot in their content, but some, for example, Ninja, who reportedly makes 1 million dollars a month, stopped cursing in his content because he realized the family friendly ads are important. So, I think the wave is coming even more over the next five years for influencer marketing opportunities.

Q: If people want to connect with you and learn more about what you do—how can they?

A: Sure, you can connect on Twitter or Instagram @alejandroreyes. Our YouTube channel is ThatReyesFamily.

An Interview with Buri the Street Dog

Did you think only people could be influencers? Not so! Although things didn't work out well for the *Yo Quiero Taco Bell* Chihuahua, things are looking great for many other canine influencers. Let me introduce you to Buri and his partner in crime, Yindi, aka @buristreetdog and @yindistreetdog. Translating for them is their owner, Samir ElKamouny, who happens to also be the cofounder of Fetch & Funnel, the ad agency we featured in Step 15.

Q: Why did you decide to create an Instagram account for your dogs, and when did you start?

A: Honestly, it started as a joke less than a year ago to prove I could grow the account fast with a minimal amount of pictures. What I didn't expect was all the influencer deals and opportunities that came along with it!

Q: What was your personal or business goal, and how have those goals worked out?

A: The goal was to get the account to 10k followers as quickly as possible and to get my dogs working with some of their favorite brands. I also wanted to promote and create awareness about the importance of rescuing dogs in need. All of these goals have been reached, and now I am working to get each of my dogs to 100k followers and to increase engagement.

Q: What is your content strategy for the account?

A: It's definitely to have the page seem authentic and true to my dog's personality. Along with that is asking questions or telling stories to boost engagement. Whenever I get a brand deal or influencer opportunity, I want to showcase the product with authenticity. I also use the platform to promote rescue dogs that are looking for their forever homes. I feel that this is a great way to give back and help dogs with similar backgrounds as mine.

Q: Is it hard to get your dog to cooperate?

A: HAHA, sometimes it is, yes. It's always the brand deals and influencer stuff that's the hardest. But then again, those are sometimes the ones that matter, so you just have to be patient, think about what you want to do, and accept the fact that it won't always work out exactly how you hoped it would.

Q: If you have influencer deals occurring, can you share the story of your first one and how that monetization method is working?

A: The first influencer deals tend to be the easiest and most fun! You just reach out to all your favorite companies and ask them to send you free stuff in exchange for posting. Larger companies will have direct contacts listed for who to reach out to for social media inquires. If it's a smaller company, just message them anywhere you can. Shoot them an email, a Facebook message, or even better, Instagram direct message. My first deal was just reaching out to my favorite dental chew company and asking if they would be willing to send me some free product in exchange for a post. They responded very quickly and then BAM—I had a box of $200 worth of breath bones on my doorstep. Once you start posting branded deals with companies, your account will then make it clear you are willing to do sponsored content. The big thing is to make sure you're still posting non-sponsored content, and to always keep it authentic. One other awesome benefit is around the awareness piece. I partnered with a rescue in Colombia and have been using my dogs' accounts to raise money for the rescue, and to showcase adoptable dogs.

Q: When I searched for your account I saw a lot of Instagram accounts named "so-and-so Street Dog." Is this a whole industry, or are they copying you?

A: At the time I created these accounts, there were very few street dog accounts. I am not sure if my dogs have inspired the trend, but I would like to think that they have influenced others to share their stories. Owning a street dog is something that has begun trending in the last several years. Especially adopting from overseas. There are organizations all over the world, Colombia, Thailand, the list is endless. Both of my dogs @YindiStreetDog and @BuriStreetDog were street dogs in Thailand that my wife and I brought home with us. I don't know if anyone out there is copying us, but it's a great group to be a part of.

Q: Are there other types of "nonhuman" accounts that you think would work well for doing something similar?

A: Yes, absolutely. As long as there is a niche, passion, or following for anything, you can photograph it and tell a story. I have an account where I just post pictures of hotels. Just photos of amazing hotels, grew the account, and now get free nights at hotels when I travel. You can create an account about anything you can think of and make it interesting, just look at @alfreddrinkingcoffee. Who knew you could get so creative just holding up a cup of coffee!

Q: Any final ideas to share with our readers?

A: Once you've posted to your account with several photos, create an awesome collage, or video telling people how awesome your content is by making a highlight reel photo or video and why they should follow you (in text). Then email accounts in your niche with larger followings and ask for sponsored shout-outs. You'll find some inexpensive deals and jump on them, this is a way to reach much larger audiences and gain followers quickly. Now that we get brand deals, you just have to make sure they're on your terms and to lay everything out on the table (the post will stay live forever, the post will only be live for 48 hours, just an Instagram Story, a saved Instagram Story, a video, three posts over two weeks, the list goes on and on!).

I think that's an important narrative to stay true to. Create an account with high-quality content that speaks to the audience you really want to target. Try to have conversations with your followers and gain long-term dedicated followers instead of just a number.

When you do that, and stick to your original content that people followed you for, your influence will go much further. I'm gonna say it again, create content that will speak to the audience you want to target. If you're a business, and you're posting pictures of internal aspects and social company meetups, and company culture stuff, that's fine as long as you're trying to use IG as a way to recruit new employees. If you're looking for customers, that content will not sell more products or services. Post about why you're better, more information about your business, why people should be interested in whatever you're selling.

SNAPSHOT

1. Influencer marketing is a historic shift in advertising spending.

2. Becoming an influencer is a new and exciting career path.

3. Evaluate whether adding another revenue stream makes sense in your business and learn from veteran influencers.

4. Find your voice and create a fun and engaging conversational style with your audience.

Part

V

R = REFINE YOUR INSTAGRAM EFFORTS WITH TOOLS AND SERVICES

Give ordinary people the right tools, and they will design and build the most extraordinary things.

NEIL GERSHENFELD

Use Tools to Expand

*I'm going to use all my tools, my God-given
ability, and make the best life I can with it.*

LEBRON JAMES
@kingjames on Instagram

*a*n ecosystem of industrial-strength tools has grown up quickly
in support of the Instagram user experience. I've tried to mention resources throughout the book, but it seems appropriate
to devote a whole chapter to the topic. A growing number of companies have created both apps and websites that help leverage and
extend the work of Instagrammers.

While many of these are intended for the general public, as a marketer you can use these tools to help enhance your marketing efforts
in several exciting ways. You even have the opportunity to use the
tools to create new product opportunities. Of course, you should note,
while these companies use the Instagram API, they are not endorsed
or certified by Instagram.

In this chapter, we'll do a rundown of many of these tools. But
do me a favor, if you know of tools that work well that you don't see
included here, DM me on Instagram and let me know about them. I'll
add them to our Expansion Pack resources.

Business Account Management Tools

A growing industry of tools and service providers are growing up around the idea of Instagram business account management. They provide a range of services. Check these out:

- **Buffer,** https://buffer.com/. Manage your social media marketing via scheduling posts, analyzing performance, and managing all your accounts together.

- **Hootsuite,** https://hootsuite.com/. Manage all your social media in one place.

- **Sendible,** https://www.sendible.com/. Unify your social inbox, schedule, and manage content.

- **Later,** https://later.com/. Visually plan and schedule your posts.

- **Tailwind,** https://www.tailwindapp.com/. A full suite of Instagram and Pinterest utilities including smart scheduler.

- **Iconosquare,** https://pro.iconosquare.com/. Industry leading analytics to grow your Instagram and Facebook accounts.

- **Sprout Social,** https://sproutsocial.com/. Sprout Social offers a full range of management tools.

- **Crowdfire,** search in the App Store. With this app you can delete ghost followers, accounts that are bots, which helps improve engagement analytics.

- **Linktree**, https://linktr.ee/. Make your Instagram bio link do more.

- **LNK Bio,** www.lnk.bio.

- **Tap Bio,** www.tap.bio.

- **Command app,** search in the App Store. Gives you the tools to optimize, grow, and monetize your Instagram profile.

- **Gramblr,** www.gramblr.com. Gramblr is a desktop application that allows you to upload pictures or videos on Instagram. There is both a Windows and a Mac version.

It features a similar upload wizard—so that you don't need a smartphone!

- **Flume app**, www.flumeapp.com. With Flume Pro you can upload photos and videos to your Instagram account directly from your Mac.

- **INK361,** https://ink361.com. Providing insights for marketers, analysts, and brand leaders to grow engagement with their audience on Instagram.

- **HypeAuditor,** www.hypeauditor.com. Evaluate your own and other people's Instagram followers quality score and a nice range of account-related metrics. One report is available for free, then they request you pay a small amount for more.

Turn Instagram Images into Physical Products

There is a growing collection of apps and services that will turn your Instagram images into physical products. This means that your Instagram work can transcend being a social media tool and can actually be used as a physical product with your customers and prospects. What can you do with the help of these apps? Consider the following:

- **Shutterfly,** www.shutterfly.com/print-your-instagram -images. Make prints and other products from your Instagram photos.

- **Canvaspop,** www.canvaspop.com/options/print-instagram -photos/. Make prints from your Instagram photos.

- **Blurb,** www.blurb.com/instagram-facebook-books. Make books from your Instagram photos.

- **Luster,** https://luster.cc/printers/. Large-scale hashtag mosaics and printers.

- **Greetabl,** https://greetabl.com. Get greeting cards from your Instagram photos.

- **Artifact Uprising,** www.artifactuprising.com/. Make prints and other products from your Instagram photos.

- **Instagoodies,** http://instagoodies.com/. Make stickers from your Instagram photos.

- **Chat Books,** https://chatbooks.com/. Make books from your Instagram photos.

- **Fox Print,** https://www.foxprint.com/. Make books, prints, magnets, and cards from your Instagram photos.

- **Sincerely,** https://sincerely.com/postagram. Make a card from your Instagram photo and send it to anyone.

- **Stitcha,** https://stitchta.com/. Create pillows and bags from your Instagram photos.

Photo Management Utilities

If you're worried that you might lose track of all your amazing Instagram images and you want a tool to quickly export them to your desktop, then you're in luck. Consider these options:

- **Hootsuite Enhance**, search in the App Store. Allows you to create photo content that is ready to be shared across multiple platforms.

- **Snapseed**, search in the App store. A complete photo editor.

- **Layout**, search in the App store.

- **Priime**, search in the App store.

Video Editing Utilities

If you want to expand your video work, consider these options:

- **Quik by GoPro,** search in the App store.

- **InShot Video Editor,** search in the App store.

- **Hyperlapse from Instagram,** search in the App store. Hyperlapse allows you to take time-lapse videos (even while you're in motion). The built-in stabilization technology produces amazing results.

- **Boomerang from Instagram,** search in the App store. Boomerang allows you to create mini videos that loop back and forth.

- **Crop Video Square Editor,** search in the App store. Allows you to crop videos or photos to square.

Hashtag and Follower Management Utilities

If you want to speed up your Instagram work, then consider utilities that help you manage the most time-consuming aspects of the site: the hashtag process and the follower management process. Fortunately there are sites that help you with both these issues. Consider these options:

- **Instatag,** search in the App Store. Wondering how to quickly manage hashtags so the process of adding them to photos is not slow and cumbersome? Instatag is a hashtag management tool. It is a quick way to tag your Instagram photos with the most popular and relevant hashtags.

- **InstaFollow,** search in the App Store. This follower management tool lets you see who is following you, who you follow that is not following you, and who is following you that you are not following. You can quickly unfollow people with this tool if you find that they are not following you.

- **Picodash,** www.picodash.com. Converts your Instagram data to spreadsheets for easy analysis.

POWER TIP

With InstaFollow, you can regularly unfollow people who are not following you back. Use this tool to ensure you have more followers than people you follow.

Photo Editing Apps

You can edit your images right on your smartphone with a nice collection of photo editing apps. If you want to ensure that your images look just right, then use one of these apps to check them and then upload them to Instagram.

- **Adobe Photoshop Express,** search in the App Store. If you love Photoshop or Photoshop Elements, then you'll appreciate the Photoshop Express app. Not only is this app loaded with useful features, but it's free!

- **Diptic,** search in the App Store. Using this collage-style photo editing tool, you can include multiple images in one Instagram photo.

Google Analytics

Your Google Analytics (GA) account, if connected to your website, can provide a very solid collection of data points related to mobile traffic and visitors from Instagram. Answer questions such as,

- How many people come from Instagram to your website in a specific time period.

- What they do in terms of pageviews, time on site, bounces, conversions.

- How this compares to traffic from other sources such as Facebook and Pinterest.

- The percentage of Instagram users visiting the website version of your Instagram versus the mobile version.

- The conversion path they take to purchase an item.

- The number of visits it takes before they convert to a customer.

- The value of their transactions.

- The percentage that use Windows, iOS, or another operating system.

- Gender, age range, city, and continent.

The data is almost endless. The most important questions include whether your Instagram visitors are converting into customers—and at what rate compared to other social sites. This will give you a good guide to understanding how to invest in the platform.

Classic Advertising Resources

Some of the books you'll want to add to your library and study include:

- Eugene Schwartz, *Breakthrough Advertising*

- David Ogilvy, *Ogilvy on Advertising*

- Claude Hopkins, *Scientific Advertising*

- Gary Halbert, *The Boron Letters*

- John Caples, *Tested Advertising Methods*

- Robert Collier, *The Robert Collier Letter Book*

- Joseph Sugarman, *The Adweek Copywriting Handbook*

Current Advertising Resources

I'd recommend following these proven leaders:

- Digital Marketer, www.digitalmarketer.com

- Adweek, www.adweek.com

- AdAge, www.adage.com

- Social Media Examiner blog and podcast, www.socialmediaexaminer.com

- MarketingProfs blog, www.marketingprofs.com

- Neilpatel.com

- HubSpot blog, https://blog.hubspot.com

- Shareaholic blog, https://blog.shareaholic.com

- Marketing School Podcast with Neil Patel and Eric Siu, on iTunes.

- Conversioncast Podcast, on iTunes

- Smart Passive Income with Pat Flynn, on iTunes

- Perpetual Traffic Podcast, on iTunes

- Call to Action Podcast, on iTunes

- Social Pros Podcast, on iTunes

SNAPSHOT

1. Third-party apps and websites can substantially improve your Instagram work.

2. Use them to effectively edit your images, manage your account, and integrate Instagram into your website and Facebook account.

3. Consider creating a collection of physical products based on your Instagram work for profit and customer cultivation purposes.

4. Use Google Analytics as the backbone of your Instagram analysis to determine the economic value of your Instagram work.

Get Coaching and Ongoing Training

A coach is someone who tells you what you don't want to hear,
Who has you see what you don't want to see,
So you can be who you have always known you could be.

TOM LANDRY

The final step in your journey is to keep learning about Instagram marketing. Two things are happening that make this a requirement. First, smart marketers are continuously coming up with new methods. Generally, these begin to get replicated and documented on blogs and in books. Second, Instagram continues to expand functionality in exciting ways. Maybe it's about to release a new feature that will unlock your ideal marketing opportunity.

In this chapter, we'll explore options related to quality online blogs, online training courses, events to consider attending, and getting small group coaching. Let's tackle them in order.

Terrific Blogs to Consider

Many readers will be familiar with these, but let me mention a few blogs that I've personally found to be very helpful. They regularly publish articles, special reports, and downloadable training content on Instagram and related topics. I'd encourage you to check them out.

- **Social Media Examiner,** https://www.socialmedia examiner.com
- **Influencer Marketing Hub,** www.influencermarketing hub.com. In addition to solid blog articles, this site has a really nice collection of resources including:
  - Instagram Hashtag Generator
  - Fake Followers Spotter Tool
  - Sponsored Post Calculator
  - Micro Influencers vs. Celebrities Comparison tool
- **Buffer's Social Blog,** https://blog.bufferapp.com
- **Tomoson,** https://blog.tomoson.com
- **Marketing Land,** www.marketingland.com
- **Sprout Social,** www.sproutsocial.com
- **Marketing Tech Blog,** https://martech.zone
- **Hub Spot,** https://blog.hubspot.com
- **Tech Crunch,** https://techcrunch.com/social/
- **Sue B. Zimmerman**, https://suebzimmerman.com
- **Later,** https://later.com/blog/
- **Hootsuite,** https://hootsuite.com/instagram
- **Neil Patel,** www.neilpatel.com

Instagram Related Training Courses

- **Get the Instagram Power Expansion Pack, companion videos, and masterclass.** In addition to the Expansion Pack resources at www.winning.online, we've also got a set of companion videos available as well as video-based training. We'd love to have you jump in and go deeper with us. Join our tribe and start learning in a community of incredible e-commerce professionals.

- **Udemy courses**. Visit https://www.udemy.com/topic /instagram-marketing/. At the time of this writing there are over 140 Instagram Marketing courses on the platform. I'd encourage you to check them out. I personally use and recommend Udemy for online courses for several reasons. First, it is the go-to learning platform for over 25 million students and 30,000 instructors. Second, courses are affordable and frequently on sale. Don't get ripped off by online charlatans pitching you expensive Instagram training, go to Udemy instead. Third, the courses are rated and reviewed, so you can see honest, unbiased feedback from actual students. In this way, instructors' courses are in a gladiator ring and the strong rise to the top. Fourth, courses are frequently updated and/or replaced by newer, better alternatives. Total side note, I'm honored to be one of Udemy's most popular E-commerce Instructors. You can check out all my courses at https:// www.udemy.com/user/jasonmiles3/.

Events to Attend

Attending social media conferences is a fantastic way to network, get training, and have a good time, too. They can also be a great way to learn about new industry trends. Look into:

- **Social Media Marketing World,** https://www.socialmedia examiner.com/smmworld/. The biggest event of its kind with 7,000 attendees annually. SMMW is a powerful annual event.

- **Social Media Camp,** https://socialmediacamp.ca. Canada's largest social media conference, and located in the cutest city on the west coast, Victoria BC, Social Media Camp is a fun conference. I've been honored to speak at it several times, and it's always fun.

- **Social Media Strategies Summit,** https://socialmedia strategiessummit.com.

- **Content Marketing World,** www.contentmarketing world.com.

- **American Marketing Association,** www.ama.org/events -training/Conferences.

Create Your Own Mastermind Group

If you can't find a coach you like, then find a friend who is also trying to master Instagram and begin working with him or her. Create your own Instagram marketing mastermind group. Use this book as a resource, and check out my other books, *Pinterest Power* and *YouTube Marketing Power*. Regardless of whether you're just starting out or you have a huge Instagram following, gathering a peer group will give you fresh ideas and help you clarify and strengthen your Instagram marketing work.

An Interview with My Coach, Brendan Burns

This conversation is with my coach, Instagram influencer Brendan Burns @brendanhburns on Instagram (Figure 19.1). I asked him to share his journey, and I think it demonstrates the importance of getting a coach as you move forward. Investing in yourself will pay dividends and give you the support, guidance, and accountability to turn your ideas into success.

Q: What brought you to Instagram?

A: I was working for a hedge fund in New York City, and while the pay was lucrative, the work was monotonous and unfulfilling. One day, while doing a session with my business coach, he shared that he had just started earning enough money from Instagram to quit his day job. In fact, he was planning to move to Los Angeles to become a full-time Instagram influencer. My coach encouraged me to look into Instagram and set up an account to share my travel pictures, something I was very passionate about. He knew that I had spent a semester of college in Barcelona, Spain, and that I had hopped around Europe and saved all the pictures that I took along the way. So I began posting those images along with newer pictures of me traveling to countries like Cuba, India, and Japan, and my Instagram account began to grow rapidly.

Simultaneously, I began investing in myself by attending self-improvement and business coaching seminars. I began to authentically share the content that was helping me grow my account and my followers, which allowed my Instagram account to grow even faster.

Figure 19.1 Brendan Burns

Q: When did you realize you could make money as an influencer?

A: As I continued to work with my business coach, my Instagram account @brendanhburns continued to grow. I began receiving collaboration requests from restaurants, hotels, and other businesses located here in New York City, and he coached me through the whole process. He taught me how to develop my very own media kit, how to position my offering, and most importantly, how to add value to the companies that I would be working with.

In the early stages of this journey, when I only had a few thousand followers, restaurant owners began contacting me to come into their restaurants for free meals. *(Note: always ask for a +1 and bring a photographer or friend!)* Eventually, these requests became so frequent that I began requiring a payment in addition to the free meal in order for the business to receive a sponsored Instagram post and/or story. As my coach advised me, I stayed focused on delivering value to the restaurants and other businesses that I worked with. I improved my photography skills, invested in high-quality gear including a Sony a6000 mirrorless camera, and would offer the restaurant raw still images to use for their own marketing purposes as a sign of goodwill and way to add value to our collaboration.

As my account began to grow, Instagram did as well. The term "Instagram influencer" was coined and a marketplace developed for sponsorships, brand deals, and paid posts that I have been fortunate to take part in. My coach encouraged me by saying that I would begin getting free meals, then free hotels, free travel, and eventually get paid to do all of the above. I was skeptical initially, but very fortunate to have had a mentor walk me through this process that resulted in success.

Q: What was your first influencer deal, how did it come together, and how did you get it?

A: My first influencer deal was with a salad chain that I love based here in New York City. Their corporate social media marketing department reached out to the email address on my Instagram profile. When they contacted me, I was already familiar with their products and was excited to work with them. I wanted to make the most of this opportunity, and I negotiated for a higher payment, which they agreed to, and I ran a sponsored post for one of their new salads. They also gave me a coupon code that I could share with all of my Instagram followers to receive a discount. I remember receiving tons of direct messages the day the post went live from my followers saying, "Thank you Brendan, I just used the coupon code!"

As a business coach myself, I coach my clients and students on the importance of displaying a professional email address (i.e., not a Gmail email address) on your Instagram profile. It gives PR agencies and companies the ability to easily reach out and adds a level of legitimacy to your brand and often results in getting contacted much more frequently.

Q: How did you scale up from that point to where you are today?

A: Over time, I continued to work with my business coach to hone my niche, share authentic content that resonated with my target audience, and build my brand. My Instagram account began to grow and I launched a website and podcast, *The Brendan Burns Show* on iTunes, as well. I learned how to add more value to the companies I partnered with. As I continued to improve my photography skills, offering raw images and videos in addition to sponsored posts resulted in larger payments and more referrals.

On top of increasing the number of sponsored posts I did and how much I got paid for them, I developed my own products and services, becoming a coach to teach interested students, entrepreneurs, influencers, and companies how to leverage Instagram as a platform to drive traffic and monetize their accounts and businesses.

The two main products I've focused on are online courses and coaching focused on entrepreneurship and personal development, topics that I am very passionate about. Through my journey, I realized that in order to cope with a traumatic past, I dove into my schoolwork as a way to escape reality. Getting undergraduate, MBA, and law school degrees from Cornell University and spending several years working on Wall Street in various banking and hedge fund roles was chasing a life that wasn't deeply fulfilling. Learning more about myself and documenting this journey as a way to help others has been very rewarding. The best part is these topics are in line with my Instagram niche, and sharing this content has allowed me to organically self-promote my products and monetize my account.

Q: Where do you see your influencer work going in the next few years?

A: I am very passionate about entrepreneurship, personal development, and self-improvement. Overcoming anxiety and unhappiness in my previous jobs in finance helped me to realize that I can inspire and motivate people to create a life that they are passionate about. Instagram is a great tool for me to share my message and grow my offerings. I plan to use Instagram to promote my new coaching programs, including 1-on-1 Life and Business Coaching, as well as group programs and in-person events. I expect to share my mission and new programs. I will also continue to do influencer deals with hotels, restaurants, and companies that resonate with my brand and share my mission.

Q: How would you summarize the influencer business opportunity to someone who is interested in learning more?

A: Becoming an influencer is a great way to live your passion and do meaningful work. Being an Instagram influencer has opened up many doors for me, both on and off the platform. The one caution I have is that being an influencer is not a guaranteed ticket to free meals and gear. It requires a lot of hard work and dedication. However, if you're willing to put in the hours and be authentic to your true self, rather than create an Instagram account focused on trying to please others, you can have tremendous success.

Q: Are there any cautions you'd share—things to avoid or look out for as you work to become an influencer?

A: One of the biggest mistakes I see people make when trying to become an influencer is that too often they select their niche based on what they think others will like. Instead of thinking about what others will like, think about what you are passionate about or what you want to share with the world. With over 8 billion people on the planet, there is a large enough audience for pretty much any industry or topic that you'd like to cover. Go with what you're passionate about and remember to stay true to what you love and share that with the world.

Q: Are there any special third-party tools or other programs you use to help run your influencer business?

A: I have used several third-party tools to help run my business. Two of my most used tools are Planoly and Loomly. I use Planoly to plan and schedule out my Instagram posts and have images post automatically to Instagram directly. These tools are invaluable to my process because they allow me to batch content and schedule it way in advance. They save me huge amounts of time, freeing me to focus on other things that will allow me to grow my influence and my brand like in-person events, speaking engagements, and coaching.

Q: What would your outcome have been if you didn't have a coach?

A: If I didn't work with a business coach, I would not have even gotten involved on the Instagram platform. My coach was aware of emerging online business and social media trends and pushed me to set up and grow an Instagram account.

Even if I had found Instagram, I would not have had success early on without having a mentor to guide me. My coach was instrumental in helping me select my niche and create content that was much more likely to go viral. He helped me brainstorm relevant accounts and made personal introductions to like-minded influencers with large followings in his network to provide me with further guidance, support, and even shout-outs.

By far the most important thing that my coach provided me with, though, was the fact that he had done it himself. When I work with my coaching students today, it is a win-win because I am teaching them to do exactly what I have done myself. I have grown my account, created the high-quality content that resonates with my followers, and I have networked with influencers all over the world. Having been able to monetize my account and passion using Instagram and being able to make a higher income now than I did while working on Wall Street positions me to share my blueprint for success with my students.

Q: How do I know if a coach is right for me?

A: Working with an Instagram coach is like working with a personal trainer. You can read as many books as you want about weight lifting, but until you hit the gym and work out with someone experienced who has already accomplished what you're looking for, it will take a lot more time to get the results you want. More importantly, when I first started working with a personal trainer, he made many corrections to my fundamentals, which saved me in the long run from making mistakes. Very often, people looking to grow on Instagram damage their brand or make other mistakes that will come back to haunt them in the long run. As Warren Buffett says, the best investment you can make is in yourself.

Q: For someone who wants a coach, how can you help?

A: I provide coaching through two primary outlets. The first is One-on-One Coaching where I work personally with individuals on growing their Instagram account, following, engagement, personal brand, and monetizing their accounts. More information on that can be found at www.brendanhburns.com.

I also provide group coaching through my Flagship Mastery Academy program, which includes my Instagram Training. This is where I hold biweekly coaching calls with my students, provide them with personal guidance, and hold my students' hands as they grow their Instagram accounts and work towards their goals. You can learn more www.winning.online.

SNAPSHOT

1. Be sure to download the Expansion Pack at www.winning .online to get all the bonus resources mentioned in this book.

2. Get ongoing Instagram training at Udemy.

3. Consider adding a social media marketing event to your calendar each year.

4. Consider joining the small group coaching program that I participate in.

5. Create your own Instagram marketing master-mind group.

Conclusion

The only question remaining is, *Can you put down this book and successfully create a powerful Instagram marketing strategy to connect with your tribe?* It is not an exaggeration to say that the success of your business may very well depend on it. Transitions to new platforms are a hard nut to crack, but they carry the seeds of new opportunities. Every time something new comes along, we all have to make a choice—do we embrace it, start with a beginner's mind, learn how to use it, and jump in? Or does the future pass us by?

Charlie Chaplin vs. John Gilbert

There was a massive transition in another industry almost a hundred years ago. It might provide a helpful lesson. In 1927, movies went from silent form to talkies. Introducing sound was a big deal. That transition had a direct impact on the actors involved, just like the rise of Instagram is having a direct impact on all marketers today.

Film critics seem to agree that it is a longstanding Hollywood myth that the transition to talkies killed the careers of the silent-era actors. Countless critics, such as Gary Susman of the *Moviefone* blog, have pointed out that many actors made the transition very nicely.

But it is also true that many larger-than-life stars did not make the transition. Many stars had acquired enormous success in the silent movie era but were ultimately rejected by audiences in the new talkie era because their voices were not well suited for the medium. Many had surprising accents or voices that simply didn't seem believable.

One very prominent silent movie star, John Gilbert, was famous for having his first talkie film present his voice in such a high pitch that audiences were shocked. Later, the audio technicians took full responsibility and said that his voice was presented incorrectly due to their technical difficulties with the new audio recording technology. He went on to do a few more talkies, but his career never recovered. His talents in the silent era generated a very large following, but those fans drifted away because of his inability to cross over into the new format.

Then there was Charlie Chaplin. Chaplin was a huge star of the silent era. He cofounded United Artists, a business that gave him complete control of his films. He would write, direct, produce, edit, score, and star in his movies. By 1918, he was one of the wealthiest men in the world. But even well into the talkie era, Chaplin refused to make the transition. He didn't support the new format and was uninterested in working with it. He continued to release silent movies throughout the 1930s, and he didn't release his first talkie until 1940, more than a dozen years after the talkie era started. His first talkie, *The Great Dictator*, was a hit—in fact, it was his most commercially successful film. Even though he was late to make the transition, when he did, he did it with perfection. He spent massively and ensured that his first talkie was a great movie. Sadly, though, over the decade of the 1940s, Chaplin fell out of popular appeal with U.S. audiences. His reign as a top star was over. The transition proved difficult even for him.

So did talkies kill the careers of silent movie stars? No, not really. What really happened was pretty simple. The stars that were fresh, young, and energetic made the leap from silent movies to talkies and went into the new era with enthusiasm. Many of them became the superstars of the next era. Sadly, the stars that were generally older and had more well-known brands were also tired and battling personal demons. They didn't make the transition well. It was a gulf they couldn't cross. Chaplin, because of his great wealth and incredible perfectionism, was able to bridge the gap, but even his influence significantly declined in the coming decade.

Four Types of People

So our cautionary tale has four types of people:

1. Fresh young actors ready to jump into the new format. They were not marquee names yet, but they would become the stars of the new talkie format.

2. Older established stars, like John Gilbert, who had extensive followings and marquee names. But "technical difficulties" sabotaged their ability to enter the space.

3. Established stars who were very prominent in the silent era, were tired, tied to the old ways, hampered by personal demons, and unable to re-create themselves in new era.

4. Charlie Chaplin, so rich he had the ability to wait 13 years, but ultimately entered the space. His decision to wait wasn't the right approach, but he was able to buy his way out of his mistake and perform fairly well in the new format.

Which type of actor are you going to be in the drama of jumping from older platforms to a fresh Instagram-powered presentation? I sincerely wish you all the best on your Instagram and online efforts. If you'd like to stay connected, get additional resources, and learn about our latest discoveries, then be sure to stop by @mrjasonmiles on Instagram and visit us at www.winning.online. We'd love to hear from you and help you continue on your journey.

JASON MILES
Seattle, Washington

Index

Page numbers followed by *f* refer to figures.

About the Author

Jason Miles is Udemy's most popular E-commerce Instructor. He is the Adjunct Professor of Online Marketing at Northwest University in Seattle, Washington. He is the author of five bestselling books, *Craft Business Power*, *Pinterest Power*, *Instagram Power*, *YouTube Marketing Power*, and *We Are Sew Powerful*.

Before becoming a full-time entrepreneur and online instructor, Miles was Senior Vice President of Marketing, Fundraising, and HR at Northwest University in the Seattle area.

In 2008 Miles started his online selling efforts with his wife at their kitchen table, and in 2013 they launched Pixie Faire, a marketplace in the sewing niche. Pixie Faire has been featured by Shopify as one of the most popular case studies on its blog. Based on worldwide site traffic it is frequently in the top 1,000 of all Shopify sites, out of over 650,000.

Jason holds a graduate degree in business administration and an undergraduate degree in organizational management. His work has been featured in *Forbes*, *The Huffington Post*, *Wharton Magazine* (of the University of Pennsylvania School of Business), IBM's Connect Chat, CNET, MSN's Business on Main, Social Media Examiner, ProfNet, PRNewswire, and other premiere publications.

Jason and his wife also cofounded Sew Powerful, a charity designed to combat extreme poverty in Lusaka, Zambia, by creating jobs for adults that focus on making purposeful products—items designed to enhance children's academic success. Things like school uniforms, reusable feminine hygiene pads, soap, and farm-fresh food for school lunches. Last year they directly impacted nearly 7,000 children and employed 25 adults.

He's sold millions online, but he's most passionate about helping people—about purpose beyond profit and creating economic power to change lives for the better.